Global Forum on Transparency and Exchange of Information for Tax Purposes Peer Reviews: Morocco 2016

PHASE 2:
IMPLEMENTATION OF THE STANDARD IN PRACTICE

November 2016
(reflecting the legal and regulatory framework
as at March 2016)

OECD
BETTER POLICIES FOR BETTER LIVES

This work is published on the responsibility of the Secretary-General of the OECD. The opinions expressed and arguments employed herein do not necessarily reflect the official views of the OECD or of the governments of its member countries or those of the Global Forum on Transparency and Exchange of Information for Tax Purposes.

This document and any map included herein are without prejudice to the status of or sovereignty over any territory, to the delimitation of international frontiers and boundaries and to the name of any territory, city or area.

Please cite this publication as:
OECD (2016), *Global Forum on Transparency and Exchange of Information for Tax Purposes Peer Reviews: Morocco 2016: Phase 2: Implementation of the Standard in Practice*, OECD Publishing. *http://dx.doi.org/10.1787/9789264261044-en*

ISBN 978-92-64-26105-1 (print)
ISBN 978-92-64-26104-4 (PDF)

Series: Global Forum on Transparency and Exchange of Information for Tax Purposes Peer Reviews
ISSN 2219-4681 (print)
ISSN 2219-469X (online)

Corrigenda to OECD publications may be found on line at: *www.oecd.org/publishing/corrigenda*.

Table of Contents

About the Global Forum

The Global Forum on Transparency and Exchange of Information for Tax Purposes is the multilateral framework within which work in the area of tax transparency and exchange of information is carried out by over 130 jurisdictions, which participate in the Global Forum on an equal footing.

The Global Forum is charged with in-depth monitoring and peer review of the implementation of the international standards of transparency and exchange of information for tax purposes. These standards are primarily reflected in the 2002 OECD Model Agreement on Exchange of Information on Tax Matters and its commentary, and in Article 26 of the OECD Model Tax Convention on Income and on Capital and its commentary as updated in 2004. The standards have also been incorporated into the UN Model Tax Convention.

The standards provide for international exchange on request of foreseeably relevant information for the administration or enforcement of the domestic tax laws of a requesting party. Fishing expeditions are not authorised but all foreseeably relevant information must be provided, including bank information and information held by fiduciaries, regardless of the existence of a domestic tax interest or the application of a dual criminality standard.

All members of the Global Forum, as well as jurisdictions identified by the Global Forum as relevant to its work, are being reviewed. This process is undertaken in two phases. Phase 1 reviews assess the quality of a jurisdiction's legal and regulatory framework for the exchange of information, while Phase 2 reviews look at the practical implementation of that framework. Some Global Forum members are undergoing combined – Phase 1 and Phase 2 – reviews. The Global Forum has also put in place a process for supplementary reports to follow-up on recommendations, as well as for the ongoing monitoring of jurisdictions following the conclusion of a review. The ultimate goal is to help jurisdictions to effectively implement the international standards of transparency and exchange of information for tax purposes.

All review reports are published once approved by the Global Forum and they thus represent agreed Global Forum reports.

For more information on the work of the Global Forum on Transparency and Exchange of Information for Tax Purposes, and for copies of the published review reports, please refer to www.oecd.org/tax/transparency and www.eoi-tax.org.

Abbreviations

ACAPS	Insurance and Social Welfare Supervision Authority (*Autorité de Contrôle des Assurances et de la Prévoyance Sociale*)
ADII	Customs and Indirect Tax Authority (*Administration des Douanes et Impôts Indirects*)
AMMC	Moroccan Capital Markets Authority (*Autorité Marocaine des Marchés de Capitaux)*
AML/CFT	Anti-money laundering and counter-terrorist financing (*Lutte Anti-Blanchiment/Financement du Terrorisme*)
ANCCF	Land and Property Registry (*Agence Nationale du Cadastre et de la Conservation Foncière*)
BAM	Al-Maghrib Bank (*Bank Al-Maghrib*)
BOC	Central Dispatch Office (*Bureau d'Ordre Central*)
BRR	Research and Cross-Referencing Department (*Brigade des Recherches et Recoupements*)
CDVM	Securities Ethics Council (*Conseil Déontologique des Valeurs Mobilières*)
CNSS	National Social Security Fund (*Caisse Nationale de Sécurité Sociale)*
CRI	Regional Investment Centre (*Centre Régional d'Investissement)*
DAI	Audit and Inspection Division (*Division de l'Audit et de l'Inspection*)
DAJT	Legal Affairs and Treaties Directorate (*Direction des Affaires Juridiques et des Traités)*
DAPS	Insurance and Social Welfare Directorate (*Direction des Assurances et de la Prévoyance Sociale*)

DCF	Tax Investigation Directorate (*Direction du Contrôle Fiscal*)
DCI	International Cooperation Division (*Division de la Coopération Internationale*)
DFC	Tax and International Cooperation Division (*Division de la Fiscalité et de la Coopération Internationale*)
DGI	Directorate-General of Taxation (*Direction Générale des Impôts*)
DLECI	Legislation, Studies and Cooperation Directorate (*Direction de la Législation, des Études et de la Coopération)*
DPRM	Cross-Referencing Planning and Monographs Division *(Division de la* Programmation *des Recoupements et des Monographies)*
DRI	Regional Directorate of Taxation *(Direction Régionale des Impôts)*
DRSI	Resources and Information Systems Directorate (*Direction des Ressources et du Système d'Information*)
ICE	Common Company Identification Number (*Identifiant Commun de l'Entreprise*)
OMPIC	Moroccan Office for Industrial and Commercial Property (*Office Marocain de la Propriété Industrielle et Commerciale)*
SA	Limited Company (*Société Anonyme*)
SANEC	Credit Institution Rating System (*Système d'Aide à la Notation des Établissements de Crédit)*
SARL	Limited Liability Company (*Société à Responsabilité Limitée*)
SAS	Simplified Joint-Stock Company (*Société par Actions Simplifiées*)
SCA	Partnerships Limited by Shares *(Société en Commandite par Action)*
SCCB	Centralisation of Bank Accounts Department (*Service de la Centralisation des Comptes Bancaires*)

SCFI	International Tax Agreements Department (*Service des Conventions Fiscales Internationales*)
SCS	Limited Partnership *(Sociétés en Commandite Simple)*
SERI	International Exchange of Information Department (*Service des Échanges de Renseignements Internationaux*)
SGG	Government General Secretariat (*Secrétariat Général du Gouvernement*)
SIT	Integrated Taxation System (*Système Intégré de Taxation)*
SNC	General Partnership (*Sociétés en Nom Collectif*)
TIN	Tax Identification Number
UTRF	Financial Intelligence Unit (*Unité de Traitement du Renseignement Financier*)

Executive summary

1. The present report summarises Morocco's legal and regulatory framework for transparency and exchange of information for tax purposes as well as its implementation and effectiveness in practice. The international standard, which is set out in the Global Forum's Terms of Reference to Monitor and Review Progress Towards Transparency and Exchange of Information, is concerned with the availability of relevant information within a jurisdiction, the competent authority's ability to gain access to that information, and in turn, whether that information can be effectively exchanged with its exchange of information partners.

2. In Moroccan law, information about the ownership of shares of Moroccan companies with share capital and the identity of shareholders is available on incorporation and on registration of such companies in the commercial register. This information is updated when there is a transfer ownership. However, there is no legal requirement for non-resident companies to keep information from which their owners may be identified.

3. In addition, Moroccan law allows limited companies and limited partners of partnerships limited by shares to issue bearer shares. However, the arrangements in place do not ensure that information about their owners is available under all circumstances.

4. Information about the members of partnerships and persons involved in a foundation and about foreign trusts is generally available in Morocco.

5. Accounting information is available under accounting and tax law. Legal requirements to retain accounting information apply to all persons having trader status and to all taxpayers liable to corporate tax, value added tax and tax on natural persons with professional income. Banking information is also available under anti-money laundering legislation. However, Moroccan laws do not ensure that accounting records and underlying documents are retained for a minimum period of 5 years in all circumstances.

6. The right to information and the right of inspection provided for in the Moroccan Tax Code give the Moroccan tax authorities extensive powers of access to accounting, banking information and information about the ownership

of legal entities. They are also empowered to control declarations and documents used in order to assess taxes and duties through the right of inspection.

7. Inter alia, these powers enable the tax authorities to request relevant information from any taxpayer, third party or other administration in order to assess and control taxes and duties. These information-gathering powers, which originate in Moroccan domestic law, apply to all international conventions pursuant to the principle that international conventions take precedence over domestic law. However, Morocco should monitor the implementation in practice of the new provisions relating to the right to information, which include a compulsory 30-day time limit to reply and strengthened sanctions.

8. Morocco has an extensive network of exchange of information agreements in the form of bilateral or multilateral conventions. Morocco is a signatory to the joint OECD/Council of Europe Convention on Mutual Administrative Assistance in Tax Matters and to the Convention between the states of the Arab Maghreb Union for the avoidance of double taxation and mutual assistance with respect to taxes on income.

9. Morocco currently has a network of information exchange agreements covering 122 jurisdictions, of which 56 are in force. Considering all the information exchange agreements concluded by Morocco, the country has information exchange agreements compliant with the standard with 120 jurisdictions and can already exchange information in compliance with the standard with 46 of them. However, some agreements signed by Morocco before 2014 are still not ratified.

10. Over the review period (from 1 January 2012 to 31 December 2014), Morocco has received 182 EOI requests. However, Morocco was unable to respond to all these requests in a timely manner. This situation is due to the complex organisation and inadequate steering of the EOI process and to non-documented processes and non-dedicated resources to this mission. Nevertheless, Morocco has recently approved the creation of a dedicated EOI department and an EOI manual is in the process of being written, which should improve the way EOI requests are processed.

11. Morocco has been rated on each of the 10 essential elements, and has also been given an overall rating. The rating for the essential elements are based on the analysis contained in this report, taking into account the determinations of Phase 1 and the recommendations formulated with regards to the legal framework in Morocco and the effectiveness of the information exchange in practice. On this basis, Morocco has been rated as follows: Compliant for elements A.3, B.2, C.2, C.3 and C.4; Largely compliant for elements A.2, B.1 and C.1 and Partially compliant for elements A.1 and C.5. Given the ratings for each of the essential elements taken as a whole, the overall rating for Morocco is "Largely compliant".

12. A follow-up report on the measures taken by Morocco in response to the recommendations made in the present report must be presented to the Peer Review Group before 30 June 2017 and then in subsequent years, in accordance with the procedure set out in the Methodology for the Second Round of Reviews.

Introduction

Information and methodology used for the Peer Review of Morocco

13. The assessment of Morocco's legal and regulatory framework is based on the international standard for transparency and exchange of information as described in the Global Forum's Terms of Reference and was prepared using the Global Forum's Methodology for Peer Reviews and Non-Member Reviews. The assessment is based on the prevailing laws, regulations and exchange of information mechanisms in force as of June 2016, other material provided by Morocco and information supplied by partner jurisdictions.

14. The Terms of Reference break down the standards of transparency and exchange of information into 10 essential elements and 31 enumerated aspects under three broad categories: (A) availability of information, (B) access to information and (C) exchanging information. This review assesses Morocco's legal and regulatory framework against these elements and each of the enumerated aspects. In respect of each essential element the review concludes whether *(i)* the element is in place, *(ii)* the element is in place but certain aspects of its legal implementation need improvement, or *(iii)* the element is not in place. These determinations are accompanied by recommendations for improvement of certain aspects of the Moroccan system, where relevant.

15. Recommendations are made on the practical implementation of each of these essential elements by Morocco. Each element can be given a grade, as follows: *(i)* compliant, *(ii)* largely compliant *(iii)* partially compliant or *(iv)* non-compliant. As indicated in the Assessment Criteria note, at the end of a phase 2 evaluation of a jurisdiction, an "overall" rating is given in order to illustrate the overall situation of the jurisdiction.

16. The assessment of the legal and regulatory framework for transparency and exchange of information and the relevant EOI mechanisms in Morocco was conducted by a team consisting of two expert assessors and a representative of the Global Forum Secretariat: Cintia Mariel De Angelis,

legal adviser at the International Tax Department of the Argentinean Tax Authority; Boya Ntsang Onanina Guy-René, Tax Inspector, assistant research officer at the Cameroon General Tax Directorate (Legislation and International Relations Division) and Mélanie Robert for the Global Forum Secretariat. The assessment of the implementation in practice of this legal framework was conducted by a team consisting of two expert assessors and a representative of the Global Forum Secretariat: Cintia Mariel De Angelis, legal adviser at the International Tax Department of the Argentinean Tax Authority, Aurore Arcambal, Legal Adviser to the Ministry of Finances, Trade and the Blue Economy of the Seychelles and Hakim Hamadi for the Global Forum Secretariat.

Overview of Morocco

17. The Kingdom of Morocco lies in the north-west of Africa. The mainsprings of the Moroccan economy are agriculture, extractive industries and phosphate processing, textiles, food processing, tourism and fishing.

18. Morocco had a population of 33.8 million in 2014 and an unemployment rate of 10.1% (third quarter 2015). GDP amounted to 889 billion[1] of Moroccan Dirham (MAD) (EUR 80 billion), with an annual growth rate of 4.5% and inflation of 0.4%.

General information on the legal and tax system

Legal system

19. Morocco is a democratic, parliamentary, social, and constitutional monarchy. The constitutional system is based on the separation of powers and the country has a decentralised system of local government. The legal system has moved towards the establishment of positive law based on the production of normative instruments and the hierarchy of norms: Constitution, international conventions, laws, regulations and other administrative decisions.

20. Legislative power is exercised by a bicameral parliament comprising the House of Representatives, whose members are elected for a five-year term of office by direct universal suffrage, and the House of Councillors, whose members are elected for a six-year term by indirect universal suffrage.

21. The tax system and the tax assessment base, tax rates and tax collection methods are governed by law in the same way as fundamental freedoms

1. At 9 October 2014, the exchange rate for the Moroccan Dirham and the euro was MAD 1 = EUR 0.0903.

and rights, infringements and the penalties for them, civil and commercial law, labour relations and social security, etc.

22. Matters not governed by law belong to the sphere of regulation. In principle, the prevailing laws and regulations apply uniformly throughout the Kingdom unless otherwise provided by law, as in tax matters.

23. The King is the Head of State. The King appoints the head of government and, on a proposal from him, appoints the members of the government, which exercises executive power.

24. The judiciary is independent of the legislature and the executive. There are two orders of jurisdictions:

- the judicial order, comprising the civil, criminal and commercial courts;
- the administrative order, which hears disputes between users and the administration, including the tax authorities.

25. General or specialist courts are created by statute; extraordinary courts may not be created. Specialist jurisdictions include the Court of Auditors, which exercises supreme oversight over public finances. Its task is to safeguard the principles and values of good governance, transparency and accountability. Regional audit offices are responsible for overseeing the accounts and financial management of local authorities.

Tax system

26. Morocco has both national and local taxes. They comprise corporate tax, income tax, value added tax, registration and stamp duty, customs duty and domestic consumption taxes.

27. Corporate tax is levied on the income and profits of companies with share capital, public corporations and other legal persons which conduct business for profit and, optionally, partnerships whose members are natural persons only.

28. Companies resident in Morocco are taxed on a territorial basis on income related to their activities. Companies not resident in Morocco are liable to tax in Morocco on their income of Moroccan origin. The standard corporate tax rate is 30%. A 37% rate is levied on credit institutions, finance companies, the central bank, and the Caisse de Dépôt et de Gestion and insurance and reinsurance companies. Non-resident companies are taxable in Morocco on their proceeds, profits and income from the assets they possess, the activities they carry on and the transactions they perform for profit in Morocco.

29. Income tax is levied on the income and profits of natural persons and partnerships that have not opted for corporate tax. The income concerned is professional income, salaried income, income and profits from property, income and profits from investments and farm income.

30. Natural persons domiciled for tax purposes in Morocco are liable to tax on their income of Moroccan and foreign origin. Natural persons not domiciled for tax purposes in Morocco are liable to tax only on their income of Moroccan origin. A natural person is domiciled in Morocco for tax purposes where he/she has its permanent home or the centre of its economic interests in Morocco or where he/she is resident in Morocco, continuously or not, for more than 183 days in a 365-day period. The income tax scale is progressive up to a marginal rate of 38%. Specific rates may also apply in certain cases.

31. Value added tax (VAT) is levied on industrial, craft and commercial activities, construction work and property development, professional services and imports. The standard rate of VAT is 20%, but reduced rates of 14%, 10% and 7% apply in certain cases.

Overview of the financial sector and the relevant professions

32. Over the last ten years or so Morocco has seen an overhaul of its financial system which has affected banking (2006), capital markets (the last reform was in 2013) and insurance (the new Insurance Code was promulgated in 2002).

Banking, capital markets and insurance

33. Banking activity is governed by the provisions of Act 34-03 of 14 February 2006 on credit institutions and similar organisations. Banking activity is supervised by the central bank (Bank Al-Maghrib, BAM).

34. Credit institutions are supervised by BAM, which ensures that they comply with the provisions of the Banking Act and its implementing regulations. BAM ensures that they have an appropriate administrative and accounting organisation and internal control systems and monitors the quality of their financial situation.

35. Operators on capital markets are supervised by the Securities Ethics Council (*Conseil Déontologique des Valeurs Mobilières*, CDVM), a public body created by a Dahir (royal decree), transformed into the Moroccan Capital Markets Authority (*Autorité Marocaine des Marchés des Capitaux* – AAMC) by Act 43-12 of 21 March 2013 in order to secure the CDVM's independence and strengthen its responsibility in the performance of its mission.

36. Total bank assets in 2015 stood at MAD 1 145 billion (EUR 104 billion).

Anti-money laundering

37. The legal framework for the prevention of money laundering and the financing of terrorism was introduced in Morocco in 2003 with the adoption of Act 03-03 on the prevention of terrorism and the adoption in 2007 of the Act 43-05 on the prevention of money laundering. These laws were amended and supplemented by Act 13-10 of 24 January 2011, Act 145-12 of 2 May 2013, and Act 86-14 of 4 June 2015.

38. The Act 43-05 on the prevention of money laundering led to the creation of a Financial Intelligence Unit, the *Unité de Traitement des Renseignements Financiers* (UTRF). The UTRF is Morocco's AML/CTF unit.

39. Other circulars subsequently set out the terms and conditions for exercise of the duty of care, such as the CDVM circular of December 2010, the Bank Al-Maghrib circular of 18 April 2012, the Insurance and Social Welfare Directorate (*Direction des Assurances et de la Prévoyance Sociale* – DAPS) circular of 4 July 2011 and the Currency Office circular 9/2013 of 1 August 2013, in addition to others decisions adopted by the UTRF.

40. In addition to making terrorist financing and money laundering a criminal offence, the Anti-Money Laundering Act, at Article 3, requires all those concerned (banks, notaries, financial intermediaries and other depositaries) to gather all the necessary information to identify their customers among owners of partnerships of companies with share capital.

Transparency and exchange of information

41. Morocco has been a signatory to the multilateral Convention on Mutual Administrative Assistance in Tax Matters, as amended (Multilateral Convention), since 21 May 2013, thus confirming its commitment to the effective prevention of international tax fraud and evasion. However, the Convention has not yet been ratified, but the ratification process is under way.

Compliance with the Standards

A. Availability of information

Overview

42. Effective exchange of information requires the availability of reliable information. In particular, it requires information on the identity of owners and other stakeholders in an entity or arrangement as well as information on the transactions carried out by entities and other organisational structures. Such information may be kept for tax, regulatory, commercial or other reasons. If such information is not kept or the information is not retained for a reasonable period of time, a jurisdiction's competent authority may not be able to obtain and provide it when requested. This section of the report assesses the adequacy of Morocco's legal and regulatory framework on availability of information as well as its implementation in practice.

43. The articles of association of all Moroccan companies must contain information about the ownership of shares and the identity of shareholders. Under the provisions of the Moroccan Commercial Code, all persons carrying on a commercial activity in Morocco must register in the commercial register.

44. Only *sociétés anonymes* (limited companies) are required to keep a register of shares relating to subscriptions and transfers of each category of registered shares. Nevertheless, other companies are required to amend their articles of association when shares are transferred; the amended articles of association must then be filed again and made public. Ultimately, the registration duties applicable to all disposals or transfers of shares ensure that the tax authorities have up-to-date information about the ownership of shares.

Just like Moroccan companies, when they submit their declaration of taxable income foreign companies are required to provide the administration with the identity of their 10 largest shareholders or partners, which means identity of those who hold at least 10% of company shares.

45. Although a review of corporate records did not reveal that any bearer shares had been issued or were in circulation in Morocco. Moroccan law still allows limited companies and limited partners of partnerships limited by shares to issue bearer shares, without the arrangements in place ensuring that information about their owners is available under all circumstances.

46. Information about the partners in partnerships and persons involved in a foundation is available. With regards to foreign partnerships, information on the identity of the 10 largest partners, which means at least those holding a minimum of 10% of the share of the partnership, is available. There is no provision for the creation of trusts in Moroccan law, but a trust may be administered from Morocco. Under anti-money laundering legislation, trustees, as professionals, are required to gather and keep all information whereby their clients and the beneficial owners can be identified.

47. However, there are no penalties to enforce the obligation for limited companies to maintain a share register and the obligation, for companies, to file and keep the originals of correspondence received.

48. All persons who are traders and all taxpayers liable to corporate tax must retain accounting data for 10 years. However, there are no sanctions directly associated with this requirement. Although there can be tax consequences for not retaining accounting information, the four-year limitation period does not allow to sanction failure to retain this documentation for a minimum period of 5 years in all cases.

49. Under anti-money laundering legislation, banks and financial institutions are required to know their customers and beneficial owners and to keep information about transactions carried out by their customers for at least 10 years.

50. During the review period, Morocco received 182 EOI requests from its partners. Of these requests, 78 concerned ownership information, 61 were requesting accounting information and 65 related to banking information. Most of the requests were seeking to obtain different categories of information. In their comments, the peers indicated that when responses were received from Morocco, they were satisfactory. However, 58 EOI requests from Morocco's partners, which did not concern any specific category of information, did not receive a response during the review period. The review team believe that this situation is due to the EOI organisation and the way EOI requests were processed in Morocco during the review period. Morocco has effective mechanisms for ensuring the availability of information as well

as effective supervision of these mechanisms. Lastly, the comments from peers do not suggest that information on ownership, accounting or bank accounts would not be available in Morocco, given that they received information from Morocco for all of these categories.

A.1. Ownership and identity information

Jurisdictions should ensure that ownership and identity information for all relevant entities and arrangements is available to their competent authorities.

Companies (ToR2 A.1.1)

51. Three types of company with share capital may be created in Morocco.

- An SA (*société anonyme*, limited company) – Act 17-95 on limited companies as amended by Acts 81-99 and 20-05 – is a commercial company whose members, called shareholders because they have a right represented by a transferable security called a share, are liable for the company's debts only up to the amount of their contribution. A limited company must have at least five shareholders and capital of at least MAD 3 million (EUR 271 000) if it makes a public offering of shares and MAD 300 000 (EUR 27 100) if not. In 2014, there were 27 696 limited companies in Morocco.
- Under the law on limited companies, it is also possible to create simplified limited companies (*société anonyme simplifiée*, SAS), which are companies incorporated as legal persons in order to create or manage a joint subsidiary or to create a company which will become their joint parent. The members of an SAS must have capital equal to at least MAD 2 million (EUR 181 000). In 2014, there were 42 simplified limited companies in Morocco.
- An SCA (*société en commandite par actions*, partnership limited by shares) – Act 5-96 on partnerships, limited liability companies and joint ventures as amended by Acts 82-99, 21-05 and 24-10 – whose capital is divided into shares, comprises one or more managing partners, who are traders and indefinitely and jointly liable for the partnership's debts, and limited partners, who are shareholders and are liable for losses only in the amount of their contribution.

2. Terms of Reference to Monitor and Review Progress Towards Transparency and Exchange of Information.

- There may not be fewer than three limited partners. An SCA's name may include the name of one or more managing partners and must be immediately preceded or followed by the words "*société en commandite par actions*". In 2014, there were 13 partnerships limited by shares in Morocco.
- A SARL (*société à responsabilité limitée*, limited liability company) – Act 5-96 on partnerships, limited liability companies and joint ventures as amended by Acts 82-99, 21-05 and 24-10 – is a commercial company. It is the most common form of company in Morocco, representing over 95% of companies. An SARL may be formed by a single person, called the sole shareholder, and may not have more than 50 shareholders. The capital of an SARL is set freely by the members in the articles of association and is divided into shares with an equal par value. Contributions may be made in kind. In 2014, there were 310 501 limited liability companies in Morocco.

Publication and registration formalities

52. SAs must be created by a written instrument, which may be a private or notarial deed. The articles of association must state the number of shares issued and their par value, distinguishing where relevant between registered and bearer shares (Article 12 of the law on limited companies). The articles of association must be signed by all the shareholders, either in person or by a proxy with special authorisation (Articles 17 and 18). Under Article 31, a list of subscribers stating their name, first name, address, nationality, status and profession, the number of shares subscribed and the amount of payments made by each one must be filed with the registry of the court where the company has its registered office, failing which the application to register the company in the commercial register will be rejected.

53. Two or more companies may jointly create a simplified limited company (SAS) in order to create or manage a joint subsidiary or create a company which will become their joint parent (Article 425 of the law on limited companies). An SAS is likewise created by the articles of association signed by all the shareholders (Article 427 of the law on limited companies). Article 31, under which a list of subscribers must be filed with the court registry, also applies to simplified limited companies, pursuant to Article 425.

54. Under Article 50 of the law on partnerships, limited liability companies and joint ventures, the articles of association of a limited liability company must state the name, first name and domicile or, in the case of a legal person, the name, form and registered office, of each shareholder, failing which the company is void. All the shareholders must sign the articles of association, either in person or by a proxy with a special authorisation.

55. Articles 17 and 18 of the law on limited companies, whereby the articles of association must be signed by all the shareholders, apply to partnerships limited by shares, pursuant to Article 31 of the law on partnerships, limited liability companies and joint ventures. In addition, Article 5 of the same law states that the articles of association must state the name, first name and domicile of each of the members of the companies to which the law applies, otherwise they will be void.

56. In addition, Article 1 of the law on partnerships, limited liability companies and joint ventures states that Article 31 of the law on limited partnerships applies to the companies governed by the law on partnerships, limited liability companies and joint ventures. Consequently, those companies are required to file a list of subscribers stating their name, first name, address, nationality, status and profession, the number of shares subscribed and the amount of payments made by each one with the registry of the court where the company has its registered office, failing which the application to register the company in the commercial register will be rejected.

57. The creation of a company is made public at the court of the place where it has its registered office by the filing of deeds and documents with the court registry for registration in the commercial register within three months, followed by publication in a journal carrying legal notices and the Official Bulletin within 30 days following registration (Article 17, 31 and 33 of the law on limited companies and Article 95 and 96 of the law on partnerships, limited liability companies and joint ventures).

58. Under the Moroccan Commercial Code, all natural and legal persons, Moroccan or foreign, carrying on a commercial activity in Morocco must be registered in the commercial register. Under Article 37, this requirement also applies to branches or agencies of a Moroccan or foreign enterprise and to economic interest groupings.

59. Under the Commercial Code, trader status results from the regular or professional exercise of the following activities:

- the purchase of tangible or intangible property for resale, the lease of tangible or intangible property for sublease and the purchase of real property for resale as it stands or after transformation;
- the exploration and operation of mines and quarries;
- transport;
- industrial or craft activity;
- banking, credit and financial transactions;
- fixed-premium insurance business, broking, commission and all other intermediation business;

- the operation of warehouses and general stores, printing and publishing;
- building and civil works, water, gas and electricity distribution, post and communications;
- business, travel, information and advertising offices and agencies, the organisation of public entertainment, public auctions;
- the provision of products and services;
- all operations relating to ships and aircraft and their accessories and all operations relating to the operation of ships and aircraft and maritime and airborne commerce.

60. Trader status also results from the regular or professional exercise of any activity that may be assimilated to those listed above (Articles 6 to 8 of the Commercial Code).

61. Article 45 of the Commercial Code states that the application to register a commercial company must include:

- the name and first name of members, other than shareholders and limited partners, their date and place of birth, nationality and national identity number or, for resident foreigners, the number of their registration card or, for non-resident foreigners, the number of their passport or any other equivalent identity document;
- the company name;
- its legal form;
- the company's purpose and actual business;
- the registered office and, where relevant, the places where the company has branches in Morocco or abroad;
- the names of the members or third parties authorised to administer, manage and sign for the company, their date and place of birth, nationality and national identity number or, for resident foreigners, the number of their registration card or, for non-resident foreigners, the number of their passport or any other equivalent identity document;
- the amount of the share capital and, if it is variable, the amount below which the capital may not be reduced;
- the date at which the company started and the date at which it must end;
- the date and reference number of the filing of the articles of association with the court registry. For limited liability companies, two copies of the articles of association must be filed (Article 95 of the law on partnerships, limited liability companies and joint ventures).

62. Article 50 of the Commercial Code states that any change to or amendment of the information provided on registration must be notified to the court registry within one month of the change (articles 95, 96 and 97 of the law on partnerships, limited liability companies and joint ventures). Only registration in the commercial register confers legal personality on companies (Article 7 of the law on limited companies and Article 2 of the law on partnerships, limited liability companies and joint ventures). Article 26 of the Commercial Code states that the originals of correspondence received and copies of correspondence sent must be filed and kept for 10 years as of their date.

In practice

Publication and registration formalities at the one-stop shop for company creation.

63. Pursuant to the Royal letter of 9 January 2002, 12 Regional Investment Centres (CRI, *centres régionaux d'investissement*) were created throughout the Kingdom of Morocco to perform two main duties, providing assistance with company creation and providing aid to investors. The CRI are one-stop shops for the creation of companies placed under the responsibility of the Wali of each region (local administrative authority). Some CRI may also have local branches, depending on their territorial jurisdiction. For example, the CRI of Rabat – Sale – Kenitra has two local branches at Sidi Kacen and Sidi Slimane.

64. As a one-stop shop, the CRI gathers under one roof representatives from the six administrations involved in the creation of companies in Morocco, namely *(i)* Moroccan Office for Industrial and Commercial Property (*Office Marocain de la Propriété Industrielle et Commerciale*, OMPIC), *(ii)* the Legalisation Department, *(iii)* the Registration Department and the Tax Identification Department of the Regional Directorate of Taxation (*Direction Régionale des Impôts*, DRI), *(iv)* the Commercial Court, *(v)* the the social security affiliation number (CNSS) and *(vi)* the Official Bulletin. Company creation within the CRI is facilitated by the use of a single application form and the successive completion in the same place of all the administrative procedures that need to be completed with the six administrations represented here.

65. To create a company, a series of compulsory and interdependent steps must be completed in a pre-determined order. Firstly the company creator must obtain an administrative certificate – the negative certificate – provided by the OMPIC, which certifies the availability of the requested trade name (company denomination, brand and logo where necessary). At the same time, the OMPIC allocates the company with its identification number, the Common Company Identification Number (*Identifiant Commun de l'Entreprise*, ICE)

which allows the company and all of its branches to be identified by all Moroccan authorities. The ICE is an additional identification number, similar to but not replacing the tax identification number (TIN *numéro d'identifiant fiscal*), the commercial register number and CNSS number, which are also allocated during the company creation process.

66. The second step is to register certain documents needed for the creation of the company with the representative of the Registration Department of the DRI. These include, in particular, the articles of association, the statement of subscription and payment to the share capital, the minutes of the constitutive shareholders' meeting, the lease agreement, the ownership deeds or the address certificate from a legal entity.

67. Next, the company creator must file the registration application with the CRI officer. The application should contain the duly completed and signed single application form for declaring the creation of a company, and all the required supporting documentation. The signature of the single application form has to be authenticated by the representative of the Legalisation Department. This procedure allows the signature to be fixed, but does not mean that the content of the signed application form has been approved. The fields of the single application form and the required supporting documentation vary according to the legal form of the company. However, information allowing the owners of the company to be identified is systematically required when the company is created.

68. The single application form invariably requires the following relevant information:

- information on the person making the declaration: first and last name or company name;
- information allowing the company to be identified: company name, brand name, legal form, amount of capital, main activity, address, contact details (telephone, fax, email). If it is a branch, information must also be given so that the registered office can be identified: name, address, commercial register number, including for companies whose registered office is abroad. In the latter case, the articles of association of the parent company must be translated into French or Arabic and authenticated by the representation of Morocco in the country of the parent company.
- Information allowing the directors to be identified: for a natural person, their first and last name, date and place of birth, function, nationality, ID number (national identity card number for Moroccans, registration card for resident foreigners or passport for non-resident foreigners), and address. For a legal person, the company name, the legal form of the company, its activity, the identification of its

permanent representative, its registration number in the commercial register, the address of its registered office.

- Information allowing partners or shareholders to be identified: for a natural person, their first and last names, date and place of birth, function, nationality, ID number (national identity card number, residence permit or passport) and address. For a legal person, the company name, its legal form, the company activity, identification of its permanent representative, its registration number in the commercial register, the address of the head office.
- Information on the company's branches and secondary offices in Morocco or abroad: name, address, corporate tax registration number (only for establishments in Morocco).
- Information on people related to the company: number of employees, accredited tax representative with the tax authorities, for foreign companies
- Information relating to the VAT, corporate tax and, where necessary, lump sum tax regimes.

69. The documents that must systematically and invariably be filed with the single application form for declaring the creation of a company include the negative certificate and all documents already presented for the registration formalities (articles of association, statement of subscription and payment to the share capital, the declaration of corporate governance, the lease agreement, the ownership deeds or the address certificate from a legal entity.) In addition, the articles of association of the parent company, whether it is established in Morocco or abroad, must be included when creating a subsidiary in Morocco.

70. When the registration file is complete, the CRI officer processes the registration and verifies the information included on the single application form, notably referring to the supporting documentation and especially the articles of association. This process is generally computerised within the CRI. However each CRI has developed its own operating environment. For example, the CRI of Rabat-Salé-Kénitra has a system (Icreate) which allows the company creation procedure to be dematerialised. The information on the single application form is entered into the system and the supporting documents are scanned. This means the information can be shared with the other administrations involved in company creation, the file can be followed up and, at each stage of the process, the transfer of information to the competent administration is made easier.

71. The registration file is then transferred to the representative of the Tax Identification Department (*Service de l'Identification Fiscale*) of the

DRI. The company is registered for business tax as well as in the Integrated Tax System (SIT, *Système Intégré de Taxation*) of the Moroccan DGI. The company's TIN is automatically generated and the file is transferred to the representative of the Commercial Court for registration in the commercial register. The company is allocated a registration number in the commercial register and the file is transferred to the representative of the CNSS for registration and allocation of the social security affiliation number.

72. The final stage in the process is the closure of the registration file and production of the list of identification numbers, which includes all the identification numbers for the company with the various administrations as well as the company's declaration of existence. These documents as well as the certificate of registration for business tax are given to the company creator. The creation of the company is then published by the representative of the Official Bulletin.

73. The aim of the one-stop shop is to make registering a company easier. The administrations present there are in no way relieved of their own obligations. Although the CRI may keep a physical copy of the registration files, each of the administrations involved must still respect their conservation and archiving obligations. Similarly, each of the administrations will receive a hard copy of the registration file.

Publication and registration formalities with the commercial register

74. Company creators can also undertake the various stages of creating a company directly with the respective administrations. In this case, the order of the stages outlined above must also be respected. The company creator must fill in the forms for each administration and provide the required supporting documentation, whilst also proving that the earlier stages have been completed.

75. To this end, in order to register the company in the commercial register held by the registry of the competent court (the Commercial Court or the Court of First Instance if there is no Commercial Court), the company creator must have received the negative certificate and the ICE from the OMPIC and be registered with the tax authorities, and therefore have obtained the certificate of registration for business tax and the TIN. All of these documents must be provided in order to register the company in the commercial register.

76. With regards to company creation, the registry of the competent court respects the same procedures as the representative of the Commercial Court within the CRI. The same information is collected and the same supporting documentation is required, in particular the articles of association that must have been registered with the tax administration. When registering the company in the commercial register, the clerk checks that the information in the form corresponds to that shown in the supporting documents, and particularly

in the articles of association. In addition, the clerk receives from its representative within the CRI all the registration applications made at the one-stop shop.

77. In contrast with the CRI, the competency of the commercial register is not limited to creating companies, but also includes registering all the changes that occur during the lifespan of a company. Consequently, once the company has been created, any future changes must be notified to the commercial register. This notably includes changes to the name, changes of activity, directors or registered office, an increase in capital, the transfer of shares in partnerships, SARL or SCA. Unlike for the other types of companies, the law does not require limited companies (SA) and simplified joint-stock companies (SAS) to declare transfers of shares in the commercial register. The clerk of the court receives and verifies requests for amendments to the commercial register. In 2013 and 2014 respectively, 36 049 and 39 022 requests for amendments to the commercial register were received. The clerk of the court also receives requests for removal from the register as well as annual financial statements. The clerk also strikes out companies from the register when required to do so by law.

78. The secretary-clerk of the court is responsible for ensuring the local register is maintained correctly under the control of the President of the Court or a judge designated by the President. At the end of each month, the latter verifies the compliance of all the entries made in the register, checking and initialling the register before a copy is sent with all supporting documentation to the central commercial register held by the OMPIC. The OMPIC centralises the 66 local commercial registers in Morocco. The central commercial register is computerised and can be searched by first and last name for a natural person and by company name or trade name for a legal person, or by the registration number. This information is available online via the portal www.directinfo.ma. All the supporting documentation for registration in the commercial register is retained indefinitely by the clerk of the court and the OMPIC. In 2014, OMPIC registered 35 645 companies and received 164 702 documents (articles of association, minutes of proceedings, etc.) in its role of centralising the legal documentation of companies).

79. In conclusion, the company creation procedure in Morocco and the requirement to inform the commercial register of any subsequent changes means that information on the identity of owners of partnerships, SCA and SARLs is available at the OMPIC when the company is created, during the period when it operates and once it is closed. However, for limited companies (SA) and simplified joint-stock companies (SAS), information on the identity of shareholders is available from the commercial register only when the company is created. Nevertheless, information on changes in ownership of SA and SAS over the lifetime of the company is available from the tax administration (see below).

Registered share register

80. Article 245 of the law on limited companies states that subscriptions and transfers of each category of registered shares must be entered in chronological order in a register which all limited companies must keep at their registered office. This article also applies to simplified limited companies.

81. There is no requirement for limited liability companies and for partnership limited by shares to enter subscriptions and transfers of each category of shares in a register. Under Article 58 of the law on partnerships, limited liability companies and joint ventures, however, shares in an SARL may be transferred to third parties only with the consent of a majority of shareholders representing at least three-quarters of the shares. A record of shareholders' deliberations must be kept, stating the date and place of the meeting, the name and first name of shareholders present or represented and the interest in the company of each one, the report and documents provided a summary of discussions, draft resolutions put to a vote and the outcome of the vote (Article 73).

82. With regard to limited liability companies and partnerships limited by shares, Article 5 of the law on partnerships, limited liability companies and joint ventures states that the articles of association must state the name, first name and domicile of each of the members of the companies to which the law applies, otherwise they will be void. Under Article 97 of the same law, all acts, deliberations or decisions amending the articles of association are subject to the same filing and publication conditions as set forth at Article 95 and 96. Consequently, any change in the ownership of shares entails an amendment of the articles of association, which must be filed again with the registry of the court of the place where the company has its registered office.

83. Although SARL and SCA are not required to keep an up-to-date register of registered shares, information about changes in ownership are available from the commercial register because of the obligation to register any changes as described above, and from the tax authorities as part of the registration obligations (see above). With regards to SA and SAS, respect for the obligation to keep a register of registered shares is verified as part of the audit operations carried out by the tax authorities, who can require any taxpayer to present the documents required by Moroccan law or regulations as part of its right to audit. However, in practice, the Moroccan authorities indicated that verification of the register of registered shares by tax auditors has not been systematic as in principle the tax administration has access to information on company ownership through certain tax mechanisms (see below).

Tax requirements

84. All taxpayers in Morocco, whether taxable or exempt, must send a declaration of existence within 30 days following the date either of their

incorporation, in the case of a Moroccan company, or of their installation, in the case of a non-resident enterprise, to the tax office of the place where they have their registered office or principal establishment in Morocco or of their domicile for tax purposes (Article 148 of the Moroccan Tax Code).

85. For a Moroccan company liable to corporate tax, the declaration must include:

- the legal form, company name and the place where the company has its registered office;
- the place of all establishments and branches in Morocco and, where relevant, in other countries;
- the company register, CNSS number (national social security fund number) and, where relevant, business tax registration numbers;
- the name and first names, status and address of the company's managers or representatives authorised to act on its behalf;
- the company's articles of association and a list of founder shareholders.

86. For a non-resident company, the declaration must include:

- the company name and the place where the company has its registered office;
- the place of all the company's establishments and branches in Morocco;
- the name and first names or company name, the profession or business and the address of the natural or legal person resident in Morocco that is accredited with the tax authorities.

87. Under Article 20 of the Moroccan Tax Code, companies, whether taxable or exempt, except for non-resident companies liable to flat-rate tax or non-resident companies with no establishment in Morocco, must send a tax return to the tax authorities within three months of the closing date of each accounting period. The tax return must include supporting documents, a list of which is established by regulation.

88. Finance Ministry order no. 297-88 of 6 rejeb 1408 (24 February 1988) on the supporting documents which companies are required to provide to the tax authorities with their tax return specifies which documents must be provided. They include accounting information such as detailed financial statements, inventories, fixed assets and depreciation together with the identity of the ten principal shareholders[3] (Finance Ministry order, OJ no. 3949 of 6 July 1988). However, not all information about ownership is required with the tax return.

3. Principal shareholders or partners are those who hold the largest number of shares in the company or partnership.

89. Property investment companies (*sociétés à prépondérance immobilière*)[4] are required to include a list naming all their shareholders with their tax return (Article 20 of the Moroccan Tax Code).

90. Registration formalities and duties also apply to verbal or written agreements, in the form of private or notarial deeds, relating to transfers *inter vivos*, free of charge or for valuable consideration, such as the sale, gift or exchange of shares in economic interest groupings, shares in companies not listed on a stock exchange and shares in property companies or property investment companies (Article 127 of the Moroccan Tax Code). Such transfers are liable to compulsory registration duties, whether they are verbal or written and whatever the form of the instrument by which they are ascertained. Under Article 128 of the Moroccan Tax Code, transfers must be registered and duty paid (4% of the transfer price) within 30 days.

91. Consequently, through the registration formality the tax authorities are constantly informed of changes to the shareholders of all companies with their registered office in Morocco, in particular where the companies are not quoted on the stock exchange. Where the instrument transferring the shares is exempt from registration duty, the parties to the instrument must submit it to the relevant registration office in order for it to be formalised free of charge (Under Article 136-III of the Moroccan Tax Code).

92. Article 211 of the Moroccan Tax Code states that taxpayers are required to keep all documents provided for by the prevailing laws and regulations for ten years at the place where they are taxed.

In practice

93. In Morocco, tax registration is a prerequisite for registering the company in the commercial register. Registering taxpayers with the tax authorities can be done either at the CRI as described earlier, or directly with the Tax Identification Department of The DRI. In both cases, the tax officer respects the same procedures.

94. Registration with the tax administration requires the taxpayer to have submitted their duly completed declaration of existence and the required supporting documentation. The fields to be filled in and the supporting documentation are the same as those described above in the section on the CRI. Once the complete registration file is submitted to the tax identification

4. Property investment companies (*sociétés à prépondérance immobilière*) are companies incorporated under one of the legal forms available in Morocco. Property investment company's main activity is to hold real estate (at least 75% of the value of its assets).

department of the DRI, all the information therein is entered into the SIT system in order to create the electronic taxpayer file:

- Taxpayer identity: legal form of the company; first and last names, and nationality for a natural person, company name and trade name for an entity; numbers of identity documents;
- Taxpayer identification: TIN, ICE, CNSS number and commercial register numbers, property deeds number and business tax registration number;
- Tax regime: type of taxation, VAT regime, date and place of creation, main activity and secondary activities, start and end dates of the fiscal year, whether or not the company receives any specific exoneration;
- Identification of directors: first and last names, address, telephone number, email;
- Identification of partners or shareholders: first and last names or company name, identity document number, TIN, full address, telephone and fax number(s), email, whether they are mains partners or not, and for shareholders only, their profession;
- Bank account details and contact details of the responsible local tax department.

Although the SIT system was put in place in 2007, it contains all information about Moroccan taxpayers, including those that pre-date its implementation. The Tax Identification department retains all the supporting documentation (articles of association, proof of tax residency, negative certificate, etc.) provided by the taxpayer in a physical file. The electronic and physical files are retained indefinitely, including if the taxpayer is delisted.

95. The SIT system allows the tax administration to hold information in its database on the owners of companies with share capital or partnerships from the moment of their creation. Each year, the declaration of existence is verified though a census of business taxpayers, under Article 17 of Law no. 47-06 relating to local government taxation. The census is performed at a local level by the Census Committee which has to include an official from the tax authorities and a representative of the municipal tax services. It covers all taxpayers carrying out a professional activity, even when they have been exempted from paying the business tax. The exempted taxpayers must provide the tax administration officer with the following information: the type of professional activity carried out, the number of employees, and the location of premises occupied. As a result of this, the tax administration is able to identify companies that had failed to respect their obligation to register with the tax authorities. In addition, the tax authorities may use its

right of inspection as included in Article 210 of the Moroccan Tax Code to establish the existence of professional activities exercised in breach of the obligation to register for tax purposes. Lastly, Article 18 of the law relating to local taxation allows tax administration officers to visit, premises being used for a professional activity at any time of the year, but during legal hours, in order to make any useful observations and gather any information needed to determine the business tax base;

96. The tax administration also has exhaustive and up-to-date information on company ownership. On the one hand, companies with share capital and partnerships are required to provide the tax administration with a breakdown of share capital when submitting their tax return. To this end, a table must be provided with the following information for each of the 10 principal shareholders or partners: first and last name or company name, address, the number of shares held during the previous and the current tax year, the nominal value of each share, and the amount of capital respectively called-up, subscribed and paid-up. This information is automatically included in the SIT system when the taxpayer makes their tax return online. This obligation to fill online the tax return will be extended to all taxpayers in 2017, but currently it concerns *(i)* companies whose turnover is equal to or greater than 10 million MAD (EUR 900 000) not including VAT, and *(ii)* taxpayers carrying out certain liberal professions. However, when a paper tax return is filed, the table showing the distribution of social capital as well as all the other documents in the file, is retained in the physical file of the taxpayer. Nevertheless, the respect of this declarative obligation does not mean that all the owners of a partnership or the shareholders in a company are known, when there are more than 10 shareholders or partners.

97. However, property investment companies are required to provide with their tax return a list of all shareholders or partners. A table must be provided containing the following information for each of the holders: first and last name or company name, national identity card or residence permit number or TIN, address, number of shares held, nominal value of the shares. This information is embedded in the SIT system either directly in case of online declaration or after being entered in the system by the competent tax officer.

98. On the other hand, any transfer of shares in economic interest groupings, partnerships, companies not listed at the stock market or property investment companies must comply with registration formalities. This obligation means that exhaustive and up-to-date information is available on the ownership of these entities. Taxpayers must deposit share transfer forms with the registration office (*bureau de l'enregistrement*) of the DRI. The tax officers will successively: *(i)* study the documents filed, *(ii)* enter into SIT identification data related to the registration office, to the transferor and the transferee, and

to the transferred shares, *(iii)* liquidate registration and stamp duties, *(iv)* take the payment and, finally, *(v)* indicate that the information has been registered on the copies of the registered documents, one copy of which is indefinitely archived in the registration office. The information that is entered in the SIT system during the registration procedure is the following:

- The identification of the company the shares of which are transferred (TIN, company name, address);
- The identification of the transferor and the transferee (TIN, first and last name or company name, identity number, address);
- The nature of the document (notarial or private deed) and a summary of the content of the transfer (date of the transfer, number of shares, disposal price, stamp duty to be paid, registration number)

Over the review period, 9.064 transfers of shares were registered in 2012, 9.542 in 2013 and 6.836 in 2014.

99. In addition, when the share transfer is carried out before a notary, the registration process can be dematerialised. An electronic data transmission system was put in place in 2015, between the Tawtik system developed by the Order of Notaries and the SIT system of the tax administration. Its use has become widespread amongst notaries. Consequently the information entered by notaries in the notarial deed is directly transferred into the SIT system.

100. In conclusion, exhaustive and complete information on the ownership of companies in Morocco is available in the databases and files of the tax authorities from the moment the company is incorporated, and this information is updated via the registration formalities. The tax administration also has the means of cross-checking information on the ownership of companies as a result of the requirement for companies to provide with their tax return both the identity and the entitlement of their 10 principal shareholders or partners as well as a list of the recipients of dividends paid by the company (see below).

Companies governed by the law on offshore financial centres

101. It is possible in Morocco to create offshore holding companies or offshore banks in Tangiers, in application of Act 58-90 on offshore financial centres. Companies governed by the Act are eligible for tax benefits. Offshore banks are liable to a 10% tax or a lump sum tax for a maximum period of 15 years (under Article 18); offshore holding companies are eligible for the lump sum tax for a period of 15 years (under Article 34).

102. However, offshore companies, whether banks or holding companies, are liable to the same incorporation and publication rules according to the

legal form in which they are incorporated (the law on limited companies or the law on partnerships, limited liability companies and joint ventures will apply as appropriate). Articles 4 and 29 of the law on offshore financial centres states that whatever the form in which the company is incorporated,

> "the interested parties must submit to the minister responsible for finance the articles of incorporation of the offshore bank or holding company and a notarial deed certifying that the bank or holding company has been duly incorporated in compliance with the applicable law".

103. Consequently, information about the ownership of shares in offshore companies is available under all circumstances, in the same way as for other companies incorporated under Moroccan law. In addition, the Moroccan authorities have confirmed that companies governed by the law on offshore financial centres, although they benefit from a reduced rate of tax, are subject to the Moroccan Tax Code and to all the obligations arising therefrom. The shares of offshore banks are exempt from the registration duty provided for in the Moroccan Tax Code (Article 17 of the law on offshore financial centres), but the parties to an exempt instrument must submit it to the relevant registration office for it to be formalised free of charge in accordance with Article 136-III of the Moroccan Tax Code.

104. In practice, information relating to the ownership of companies governed to the law on offshore financial centres is available at the time of their creation and then subsequently when there are any changes in shareholders or partners, from the tax authorities or the commercial register, under the same conditions as other companies registered under Moroccan law. There have been no comments from peers suggesting that information on the ownership of offshore companies would not be available in Morocco.

Foreign companies

105. Foreign companies carrying on a commercial activity in Morocco are subject to the same formalities for registration in the company register as Moroccan companies. The same applies to Moroccan branches on foreign companies (Articles 37 and 41 of the Commercial Code). The information to be provided to the registry for registration purposes is the same as for Moroccan companies. However, the content of the articles of association will be determined by the legal requirements of the jurisdiction where the company was incorporated, and information on the ownership of shares will be available only if that is a requirement in the said jurisdiction.

106. Foreign companies and Moroccan branches of foreign companies are also required to notify any change to the information provided on registration, by application of Article 50 of the Commercial Code.

107. In accordance with the territoriality principle, non-resident companies are liable to tax in Morocco on the proceeds, profits and income from the assets they possess, from the business they conduct and from the transactions they carry out for profit in Morocco, even on an occasional basis, and on proceeds, profits and income taxable in Morocco under the provisions of tax conventions (Article 5 of the Moroccan Tax Code).

108. Foreign companies liable to corporate tax (on income from commercial activities in Morocco, profitable operations realised in Morocco or on income from properties held in Morocco – Article 5 of the Moroccan Tax Code) must identify themselves to the tax authorities within 30 days following their installation or the start of their activities in Morocco. In order to do so, they must file a declaration of existence (Article 148 of the Moroccan Tax Code). Foreign companies, except for non-resident companies liable to flat-rate tax or non-resident companies with no establishment in Morocco, must file an annual tax return in the same way as Moroccan companies (Article 20 of the Moroccan Tax Code). As mentioned above, companies with share capital and partnerships, including foreign companies, are required to provide to the tax administration, in support of their tax return, the identity of their 10 principal shareholders or partners[5] (Decree from the Ministry of Finances, Official Bulletin no. 3949 of 6 July 1988). Although this obligation does not make it possible to identify all the owners of foreign companies, it does mean that an updated list of those holding at least 10% of stocks or shares is available. In addition to this declarative obligation, information on the ownership of foreign companies should in principle be available as a result of the anti-money laundering obligations of service providers, in particular banks. Indeed, all traders, including foreign companies, that have an economic activity in Morocco must open a bank account in a bank established in Morocco (see below).

109. Over the review period, there were relatively few foreign companies operating in Morocco, as the table below indicates. Lastly, comments from peers do not suggest that information on foreign companies with a permanent establishment in Morocco is not available.

	2012	2013	2014
Number of permanent establishments of foreign companies	753	897	994
– Including creations	130	144	97

5. Largest shareholders or partners means those that hold the largest number of shares in the share capital of the company.

Anti-money laundering legislation

110. In Morocco, the rules relating to the prevention of money laundering stem from Act 43-05 on money laundering, as amended and completed. Article 3 of the Act states that the persons to whom it applies are required to gather all the necessary information to identify their regular or occasional customers and beneficial owners.

111. The term beneficial owner within the meaning of this Act means any natural person on whose behalf the customer acts or, where the customer is a legal person, any natural person who ultimately controls or owns it (Article 3).

112. Under Article 2 of the Act, persons governed by its provisions are the following public- or private-law natural and legal persons:

- Bank Al-Maghrib;
- credit institutions and similar organisations;
- banks and offshore holding companies;
- financial holding companies;
- fund transfer intermediation companies;
- insurance and reinsurance companies and insurance and reinsurance intermediaries;
- financial asset managers;
- auditors, external accountants and tax advisers;
- service providers involved in the creation, organisation and domiciliation of enterprises;
- members of an independent legal profession who take part in a financial or property transaction in their customer's name and on his or her behalf, or who help their customer to prepare or carry out operations relating to:
    - the purchase or sale of property assets or commercial enterprises;
    - the management of funds, securities or other assets belonging to the customer;
    - the opening or management of bank, savings or securities accounts;
    - the organisation of the necessary contributions to constitute, manage or operate companies or similar structures;
    - the formation, management or direction of *fiducies*, companies or similar structures.

113. Where the customer is a legal person, persons governed by the Act must, by means of the necessary documents and indications, verify all information concerning its name, legal form, activity, the address of its registered office, its share capital, the identity of its managers, the powers of persons authorised to represent it with regard to third parties or to act on its behalf by virtue of a power of attorney and the beneficial owners (Article 3).

114. Article 5 further states that persons governed by the Act must:

- ascertain the identity of principals for the performance of transactions whose beneficiary is a third party;
- ascertain and verify the identity of persons acting on behalf of their customers by virtue of a power of attorney; and
- ensure that their customer files are regularly updated.

115. Under Article 4, persons governed by the Act must not execute a transaction where it has not been possible to verify the identity of the persons concerned or where the identity is incomplete or plainly fictitious.

116. In addition, Article 18 of the Commercial Code states that all traders must open an account with a bank or postal cheque centre for the purposes of their business. Consequently, there is always a person governed by the provisions of the Anti-Money Laundering Act who must ascertain the identity of the company's shareholders (Article 3 of the Anti-Money Laundering Act).

117. All documents relating to the identity of customers must be kept for ten years as of the date on which the transaction is executed (Article 7).

In practice

118. The Financial Intelligence Unit (*Unité de traitement du renseignement financier*, UTRF) is the Moroccan body in charge of combating money laundering and the funding of terrorism (AML/CTF). Under the provisions of Article 14 of law no. 43-05, the UTRF was created by decree no. 2-08-572 of 24 December 2008, and started operating on 10 April 2009. In operational terms, its role is to gather and process information relating to activity suspected of being linked to money laundering, to money laundering predicate offense or to the funding of terrorism. It transfers to the public prosecutor cases where the information gathered documents actions that are likely to constitute a breach of AML/CTF legislation. Within the context of its duties, it has a right to information from taxpayers, administrations, public establishments and public or private corporate entities. The UTRF has a staff of 25 officers and uses the UTRFnet system (go AML) which allows for an automatic data processing and provides a secure email service that currently

operates with credit establishments and should be progressively extended to other entities governed by the legislation.

119. The UTRF is the supervisory body for all entities governed by the law and supervised by no other authority, such as for example, casinos, accountants, certified accountants, estate agents and jewellers. The UTRF carries out awareness-raising actions amongst these entities in close collaboration with other supervisory authorities including:

- The Ministry of Justice for legal professions (attorneys, notaries, etc.);
- The Bank Al Maghrib (BAM) for credit establishments;
- The Insurance and Social Welfare Supervision Authority (*Autorité de Contrôle des Assurances et de la Prévoyance Sociale*, ACAPS) for insurance and reinsurance organisations and for insurance and reinsurance intermediaries;
- The Moroccan financial market authority (*Autorité marocaine des marchés de capitaux*, AMMC) for stockbrokers, securities intermediaries, the central depositary and management companies; and
- The Currency Office for foreign exchange bureaux.

120. The level of control over the respect of AML/CTF obligations by persons subject to AML/CTF obligations varies according to the supervisory authorities. Thus, in addition to the awareness-raising and guidance operations, the BAM, the AMMC and the Currency Office perform desk inspections and general or thematic inspections where these authorities ensure that the persons under their supervision respect the applicable legislation, including in AML/CTF. As an example, the AMMC has performed in 2014 11 inspections of stockbrokers and account holders, one inspection of the central depository, and eight inspections of management companies. The Currency Office performed 62 onsite inspections of foreign exchange bureaux in 2013 and 247 inspections in 2014. However, during the onsite visit, the Moroccan authorities and the professional organisations indicated that supervision by the Ministry of Justice of legal professions was not effective. With regard to credit establishments, the BAM performs effective supervision, which will be described in detail in section A.3.

121. In addition, the UTRF has effectively exercised its right to information with the administrative authorities and the entities it supervises, as shown in the table below. As a result, it submitted nine cases to the public prosecutor in 2012, 11 cases in 2013 and 16 cases in 2014.

	2012	2013	2014
Number of right to information requests served on supervised entities	1 714	1 543	4 914
Number of right to information requests served on public administrations	1 438	1 538	2 465

122. In conclusion, information relating to the ownership of companies with share capital or partnerships is generally available from persons subject to AML/CTF legislation, as a result of the effective supervision of these professionals. However, with regards to legal professions, the Ministry of Justice is not effectively monitoring compliance with AML/CTF obligations. Therefore, there is no reasonable assurance that information on company ownership would be available from these professionals. Nevertheless, this information is available, as mentioned above, from the commercial register and the tax administration.

Information held by nominees

123. The notion of nominee exists in Moroccan law. Article 879 of the Dahir on obligations and contracts defines a power of attorney as "a contract whereby one person instructs another to perform a lawful action on the principal's behalf". Article 19 of the same Dahir defines the term "contract" as "the parties' agreement on the essential elements of the obligation and all the other lawful clauses which the parties deem essential".

124. Article 926 of this Dahir also states that the principal is required to execute directly the undertakings contracted on his behalf by the nominee, within the limits of the powers conferred upon the nominee. The Moroccan tax authorities have indicated that the nominee has to indicate to third parties that he is acting on behalf of his client.

125. Section 1, Article 2 of the Moroccan Anti-Money Laundering Act includes the obligation for all those governed by its provisions to identify beneficial owners and owners of last resort among their customers or through nominees acting on customers' behalf. Nominee shareholders that are not acting by way of business are not covered under the AML provisions and thus, do not have a specific legal obligation to retain identity information on the person for whom they act as the legal owner. Nevertheless, it may be expected that such nominees do know who their client is in order to correctly perform their duties as a nominee. In addition, these nominees might establish a relationship with a financial institution in Morocco (e.g. opening a bank account to receive dividends on the shares they hold), in which case the financial institution is required to perform customer due diligence measures with respect to the person acting as nominee and the beneficial owner. In any event, the group of nominee shareholders not covered by the AML obligations would primarily consist of persons performing services gratuitously or

in the course of a purely private non-business relationship and is therefore likely to be limited.

126. In practice, there have been no comments from peers suggesting that there are inherent difficulties with the information held by nominees in Morocco. In addition, when the nominee is acting as a professional, it is subject to registration obligations with the commercial register and the tax administration, to declarative obligations with the tax administration and to AML/CTF obligations as mentioned above.

Conclusion

127. In conclusion, under the process for incorporating and registering companies in Morocco, information about the ownership of shares and the identity of shareholders at the time of incorporation is contained in the articles of association and provided to the registry of the court of the place where the company has its registered office. The same information and documents must be provided when making the declaration of existence with the tax administration. Moroccan law also ensures that such information is updated, for limited companies and simplified limited companies through the register of shareholders, and for property investment companies through the annual tax return, or for limited liability companies and partnerships limited by shares by amendment of the articles of association. Foreign companies are required when they submit their tax return to provide the administration with the identity of their 10 principal shareholders, which means the identity of those who hold at least 10% of company shares. In addition, the tax authorities are informed of any transfer of shares by means of the registration duty. Under the Anti-Money Laundering Act, persons governed by its provisions are required to identify their regular or occasional customers, all traders must open an account with a bank or a postal cheque centre and all nominees must identify their customers and beneficial owners.

128. The company registration procedure is made up of a series of successive and interdependent stages that facilitates the monitoring and supervision of the process by each of the actors involved in the process. It makes information about company ownership available when the company is being incorporated. Indeed, registration of the articles of association is a prerequisite for the declaration of existence from the tax administration which is itself a prerequisite for registration in the commercial register. The creation of the ICE and the CRI also help to ensure an integrated process and easier monitoring. The supervision of the commercial register is effective and the commercial register is centralised and computerised, with the information being retained indefinitely in both hard and digital copy format. In addition, the tax administration holds company ownership information in their own databases, in particular the SIT system, as well as their physical files. Each year, it uses its power of inspection to detect companies that have not been registered.

129. Over the lifetime of a company, knowledge of company owners, with the exception of SA and SAS, is ensured by the requirement to register any changes in the commercial register. In addition, the tax administration effectively monitors the registration formalities for all transfers of shares in companies with share capital, including SA and SAS. The information collected is recorded in the SIT system and a copy of the transfer deed is retained in the tax administration's files. In addition, the tax administration effectively monitors the obligation to declare the list of the 10 principal partners or shareholders, including for foreign companies.

130. The supervisory authorities of professions subject to AML/CFT legislation exercise their powers of supervision in practice, with the exception of the Ministry of Justice. Availability of information about the company ownership by legal professionals is not ensured. However, this information is available either from the commercial register or directly from the databases and files of the tax administration itself. Morocco should nevertheless ensure that the Ministry of Justice effectively supervises the respect of their AML/CFT obligations by the professions governed by that legislation.

131. During the review period, Morocco has received 78 EOI requests on the ownership of companies with share capital and partnerships. In their comments, the peers noted that when responses were received from Morocco, these were satisfactory. However, around 15 of these EOI requests went unanswered during the review period. Given the mechanisms that ensure the availability of companies' ownership information in Morocco and their supervision, the assessment team are of the opinion that the explanation for this situation is to be found in the EOI organisation and process in place in Morocco during the review period (see C.5).

Bearer shares (ToR A.1.2)

132. In Morocco, the law on limited companies (SA) provides for the creation of bearer shares. Limited companies and partnerships limited by shares, by application of Article 31 of the law on partnerships, limited liability companies and joint ventures, may issue bearer shares. However, only limited companies and partnerships limited by shares whose articles of association expressly include the possibility of issuing bearer shares may indeed do so (Article 12 on the law on limited companies).

133. There are certain arrangements in Moroccan law which ensure the availability of information about the identity of holders of bearer shares in specific circumstances. The Moroccan authorities have confirmed that these obligations require the identification of the legal and beneficial ownership.

- Listed shares are registered in accounts with authorised financial intermediaries in accordance with the provisions of Act 35-96 on the creation of a central depositary and the institution of a general rule for the registration in accounts of certain securities. The identity of owners of listed bearer shares can therefore be ascertained.

- With regard to bearer shares of unlisted companies, Article 3 of the Anti-Money Laundering Act requires all persons governed by its provisions (banks, notaries, lawyers, financial intermediaries and other depositaries) to gather all the necessary information to identify their customers among the owners of limited companies. They are therefore required to identify the owners of bearer shares when the company is created by a notary (where relevant) and on opening a bank account.
- Article 152 of the Moroccan Tax Code states that taxpayers who pay dividends must file a declaration with the tax authorities containing certain items of information, including the identity of dividend recipients and their address or tax identification number.

134. Transfer of bearer shares is also liable to compulsory registration duties, whether they are verbal or written and whatever the form of the instrument by which they are ascertained. Under Article 128 of the Moroccan Tax Code, transfers must be registered and duty paid (4% of the transfer price) within 30 days. Penalties are applicable for non-compliance with this obligation (Article 184 of the Moroccan Tax Code). However, it is not clear that this measure is sufficient as the tax authorities have no means to verify whether bearer shares have been transferred or not. In addition, Moroccan authorities were unable to provide statistics on the number of limited companies and limited partners of partnerships limited by shares that may issue bearer shares or the possible number of bearer shares in existence.

135. Although there are arrangements which require the availability of this information, the mechanisms in place do not ensure the identification of the holders of bearer shares under all circumstances.

136. In practice, companies authorised to issue bearer shares, namely limited companies (SA), simplified joint-stock companies (SAS) and partnerships limited by shares (SCA) represent less than 9% of companies with share capital. The Moroccan authorities have identified and verified all companies authorised to issue bearer shares in order to establish whether or not they have actually done so. The procedure they used was as follows:

- The resources and information systems directorate (*Direction des Ressources et du Système d'Information* (DRSI)) of the DGI identified all legal persons registered as a SA, SAS or SCA with the DGI. The lists of companies were drawn up and transmitted to the competent DRI for action.

- The DRI were charged with the task of identifying whether these companies had in fact issued bearer shares. Tax officers examined the documents available in the physical files of these taxpayers, in particular their articles of association, as well as the annex showing the distribution of capital in the tax return that has to be filed each year by the companies;

The DRI have reported that they do not find any bearer shares. In fact, the possibility of issuing bearer shares must be included in the articles of association for SA, SAS and SCA in order for them to be able to issue them.

137. The professional bodies met during the on-site visit, and primarily the statutory auditors, accountants and notaries, explained that they have never encountered in their professional activity situations involving bearer shares.

138. In conclusion, although a review of corporate records did not reveal that any bearer shares had been issued or were in circulation in Morocco, bearer shares can still be legally issued by SA, SAS and SCA in Morocco. Morocco has some legal arrangements which ensure the availability of information about the identity of holders of bearer shares in practice. However, these mechanisms do not ensure their identification under all circumstances. Therefore, it is recommended that Morocco should take the necessary steps to ensure that appropriate arrangements are in place to identify the owners of bearer shares under all circumstances.

Partnerships (ToR A.1.3)

139. Three types of partnership may be created in Morocco, namely *sociétés en nom collectif* (general partnerships, SNC), *sociétés en commandite simple* (limited partnerships, SCS) and *sociétés en participation* (joint ventures, SP). They are governed by Act 5-96 on partnerships, limited liability companies and joint ventures as amended by Acts 82-99, 21-05 and 24-10.

- An **SNC** is one in which all the partners are traders with indefinite and joint liability for the partnership's debts. The partnership has a name, which may include the name of one or more partners and must be immediately preceded or followed by the words "*Société en nom collectif*". Partnerships with sales in excess of MAD 50 million (EUR 4.5 million) at the end of the business year must appoint at least one auditor. Shares are nominative and may be transferred only with the consent of all the partners. There were 2 199 SNC in Morocco in 2014.

- An **SCS** comprises managing partners and limited partners. It has a name which may include the name of one or more managing partners and must be immediately preceded or followed by the words "*Société en commandite simple*". The managing partners are indefinitely and jointly liable for the partnership's debts. The limited partners are liable for the partnership's debts only up to the amount of their contribution; they may not perform any act of management. There were 132 SCS in Morocco in 2014.

- It is also possible to create a **joint venture**. This exists only in the relations between partners and is not intended to be known by third parties. It does not have legal personality and is not subject to any registration requirement or publication formality. If the company is of a commercial nature, the relations between partners are governed by the rules applicable to general partnerships, unless otherwise provided. There were 214 joint ventures in Morocco in 2014.

140. Act 5-96 on partnerships, limited liability companies and joint ventures applies to general partnerships and limited partnerships in the same way as to limited liability companies and partnerships limited by shares. As explained in Section A.1.1 on these companies, the Act provides that the articles of association must state the name, first name and domicile of each partner or, if it is legal person, its name, legal form and the place where it has its registered office, and be signed by all the partners, otherwise the company is void (Article 5 for general partnerships and Articles 21 and 23 for limited partnerships).

141. In addition, Article 1 of Act 5-96 states that Article 31 of the law on limited companies applies to the companies and partnerships governed by the law on partnerships, limited liability companies and joint ventures. Consequently, those companies and partnerships are required to file a list of subscribers stating their name, first name, address, nationality, status and profession, the number of shares subscribed and the amount of payments made by each one with the registry of the court where the company has its registered office, failing which the application to register the company in the commercial register will be rejected.

142. For general partnerships and limited partnerships, Article 15 of the law on partnerships, limited liability companies and joint ventures states that the shares are nominative and may be transferred only with the consent of all the partners (Article 27 for limited partnerships). In addition, share transfers must be made in writing, failing which they are void. They must be notified to the company in order that they may be relied on, but notification may be replaced by the filing of a copy of the transfer deed (Articles 16 and 21). They must also be published in the commercial register in order that they may be relied on against third parties (Articles 17 and 21). The provisions of these articles are confirmed in Article 195 of the Code of Obligations and Contracts, which states that in order to be relied on against third parties, transfers of corporate rights must be notified to the partnership or accepted by it in a notarial or private deed.

143. Under Article 5 of the law on partnerships, limited liability companies and joint ventures, the articles of association must state the name, first

name and domicile of each of the members of the companies to which the law applies, otherwise they will be void. The articles of association are kept at the partnership's registered office and all the partners may know the identity of their fellow-partners. In addition, any act, deliberation or decision the effect of which is to amend the articles of association is subject to the same filing and publication requirements (Article 97 of the law on partnerships, limited liability companies and joint ventures).

144. Article 26 of the Commercial Code states that the originals of correspondence received and copies of correspondence sent must be filed and kept for 10 years as of their date.

145. Joint ventures do not have legal personality. They exist only in the relations between partners and are not intended to be known by third parties. They can therefore be created *de facto* and are not subject to any registration or publication requirement (Article 88 of the law on partnerships, limited liability companies and joint ventures). Consequently, the partners are personally liable to tax on income from the joint venture and no other information on the identity of the partners is required.

Publication and registration formalities

146. General partnerships and limited partnerships in Morocco are subject to the same registration requirements under the Commercial Code as those described in Section A.1.1 for companies with share capital. As for companies, partnerships must be constituted in writing by private or notarial deed. The creation of the partnership is made public at the court of the place where it has its registered office by the filing of deeds and documents with the registry of the competent court for the purposes of registration in the commercial register within three months, followed by publication in a journal carrying legal notices and the Official Bulletin within 30 days following registration.

147. In practice, the procedure for creating and registering partnerships in the commercial register is the same whatever the corporate form of the company (see above for companies with share capital), whether the company is created via the CRI or directly at the competent commercial register. The same information and the same documents are collected during the registration procedure. This being said, for partnerships, a copy of the identity documents of all partners are gathered (national identity card for Moroccans, residence permit for foreigners and registration certificate for companies including foreign companies). As for companies with share capital, with the exception of SA and SAS, any changes made to the articles of association of a partnership must be also registered in the commercial register. Supervision of the commercial register is also identical for partnerships and companies with

share capital. In this way, information on the identity of partners in partnerships is available in practice and updated in the commercial register.

Information held by SNCs, SCSs and non-trading partnerships

Tax requirements

148. Partnerships are subject to tax law requirements in the same way as any other taxpayer. Article 148 of the Moroccan Tax Code states that all taxpayers, whether taxable or exempt, must send a declaration of existence within 30 days following the date of either their incorporation, if the partnership is a Moroccan partnership, or their installation, if it is a resident or non-resident enterprise. The information to be provided in the declaration of existence is the same as for companies as mentioned in Section A.1.1 above.

149. Under Article 2-III of the Moroccan Tax Code, partnerships whose partners are natural and legal persons or legal persons only are liable to corporate tax. Under Article 2-II, partnerships constituted in Morocco whose partners are natural persons only may opt for corporate tax; the decision is irrevocable. Otherwise, they are liable to income tax payable by the principal partner (Article 26-I).

150. Partnerships liable to corporate tax are subject to the same filing requirements as companies, as explained in Section A.1.1. They must file an annual tax return (Article 20 of the Moroccan Tax Code). The tax return must also include information about the identity of the 10 principal shareholders (Finance Ministry order, OJ no. 3949 of 6 July 1988) but a list of all partners is not required with the return.

151. Partnerships liable to income tax (i.e. partnerships constituted in Morocco whose partners are natural persons only and which have not opted for corporate tax) must complete a declaration of taxable income which is attached to the declaration of total income of the principal partner and filed with the tax authorities (Article 82 of the Moroccan Tax Code). The declaration of taxable income must include ownership information of the 10 principal partners (Finance Ministry order, OJ no. 3949 of 6 July 1988). However, the information on all the partners of the partnership is not required with this declaration. The taxable income of the partnership must be added to the professional income category of the declaration filed by the principal partner, who is liable to tax on the income (Article 26-I of the Moroccan Tax Code). The principal partner is the one who owns the largest share of the partnership. If shares are equal, the partners must decide amongst themselves which of them will be the principal partner[6] (Circular no. 171 relating to the Moroccan Tax Code).

---

6. The notion of "principal partner" is assessed with reference to the share capital except in the case of a limited partnership. The principal partner is the one who

152. If the principal partner of a partnership liable to income tax (and not corporate tax) is not resident in Morocco, he or she must file an annual tax return in Morocco and state his or her income from Moroccan sources, including income from the partnership (Articles 23-I, 25 and 82 of the Moroccan Tax Code).

153. Property investment companies must also include a list naming all the owners of their shares with their tax return (Article 20 of the Moroccan Tax Code). However, the complete list of all shareholders of the partnership is not transmitted to the tax authorities with the annual declaration of total income nor with the principal partner's declaration.

154. In practice, the availability of information on the ownership of partnerships is ensured by the same means as those that apply for companies with share capital, described earlier. The tax administration is provided with information about the partners of partnerships during the tax registration process. This information is then updated via the formality of registering share transfers. In addition, this obligation is cross-referenced with the annual tax declaration of income to which the list of the 10 principal partners must be attached. The tax administration monitors compliance with tax registration obligations in the same way for partnerships and companies with share capital.

Foreign partnerships

155. Partnerships created in another jurisdiction which carry on a commercial activity in Morocco are not under any legal requirement to keep information about share ownership. The information will be available in documents relating to the creation of the partnership only if that is a requirement in the jurisdiction where the partnership was created. The same applies to updates of such information following a transfer of shares.

---

holds the largest number of shares. The shares to be taken into consideration include not only those that are the personal property of each partner but also those that belong to their spouses, partners or minor children. Where the share capital is divided equally between all the partners, the principal partner is the one who acts as manager. Where the manager is not chosen from among the partners or where the management is entrusted to several partners, the principal partner is: *(i)* the one who, by his collaboration and active involvement in the company's administration appears to be the person most interested in the smooth operation and development of the enterprise; or *(ii)* the one who offers the best guarantee with regard to collection of tax. The characteristics of management are defined according to the company's legal form. In the event of equal shares, it is Circular no. 717 relating to the Moroccan Tax Code which defines the principal partner (p. 242). 1-2-Definition of the principal partner.

156. However, as mentioned above, partnerships, including foreign partnerships, are required to provide to the tax administration, in support of their tax return, the identity of their 10 principal shareholders or partners (Decree from the Ministry of Finances, Official Bulletin no. 3949 of 6 July 1988). Although this obligation does not make it possible to identify all the owners of foreign partnerships, it does at least mean that an updated list of those holding at least 10% of stocks or shares is available. In addition to this declarative obligation, information on the ownership of foreign partnerships should in principle be available as a result of the AML/CFT obligations of service providers. Lastly, comments from peers do not suggest that information on foreign partnerships with a permanent establishment in Morocco is not available.

Anti-money laundering legislation

157. Under Article 2 of the Anti-Money Laundering Act, certain natural or legal persons who are not members of the partnership are required to keep information on the identity of the partners of partnerships. They include banks, notaries, lawyers and all service providers involved in the creation, organisation and domiciliation of partnerships.

158. Under Article 18 of the Commercial Code, as is the case with companies, any partnership carrying on a trading activity is required to open an account with a bank or postal cheque centre for the purposes of the business. Consequently there is always a person governed by the Anti-Money Laundering Act who is required to identify the owners of the partnership and keep that information (Article 3 of the Act).

159. In practice, information on the owners of partnerships, whether they are foreign or Moroccan, should be available from persons subject to AML/CTF obligations in the same way, and with the same reservations, as outlined above with regards to companies with share capital.

Conclusion

160. Information about the owners of partnerships must be included in the articles of association and filed with the application for registration in both the commercial register and with the tax administration. Share transfers must be notified to the partnership, which must keep a copy of such correspondence. The articles of association must also be amended and published again in the commercial register so that they may be relied on against third parties. Any transfer of shares must also be registered with the tax administration. Foreign partnerships are also required to provide to the tax administration, in support of their tax return, the identity of their 10 principal partners, which means at least those who hold at least 10% of the share of the partnership.

161. In practice, information on the ownership of partnerships is available in Morocco under the same conditions as for companies with share capital. However, as indicated earlier, Morocco was not able to respond to around 15 EOI requests on the ownership of partnerships and companies with share capital due to the EOI organisation and process in place in Morocco during the review period.

Trusts (ToR A.1.4)

162. There is no provision for the constitution of trusts in Moroccan law and Morocco is not a signatory of the Hague Convention of 1 July 1985 on the Law Applicable to Trusts and on their Recognition. However, there is nothing in Moroccan law to prevent a Moroccan resident from acting as trustee or administrator of a trust created under the laws of another country.

163. In a situation where a trust governed by the laws of a foreign country is administered in Morocco, there is no specific obligation to register with the public authorities. However, the Moroccan commercial code requires all natural or legal persons, whether Moroccan or foreign, performing a commercial activity, such as a service, in Morocco to register with the commercial register, and this would be applicable to any person administering a trust created abroad. As soon as a commercial activity is started, the person acting as a trustee in Morocco is required to register with the commercial register and specify their activity. In this case, the same information and documents as are required for any trader must be submitted to the commercial register, whether at the time of registration or once the activity is underway. However, these obligations do not mean that under all circumstances the identity of the settlor and the beneficiaries will be known.

164. Similarly, as for any person performing a taxable activity, the person acting as trustee is required to register with the tax administration, providing the information and supporting documentation needed for the tax registration process. Indeed, if the trustee resident in Morocco does not reveal the identity of the person for whom the assets are being administrated, the person acting as trustee will be taxed on his global income, thus including the income from the trust (article 23-I-1 of the Moroccan Tax Code). In addition any changes of ownership, whether free of charge or for a consideration, must be registered, which allows the former and new owner of the assets of a foreign trust to be identified, when the assets are located in Morocco.

165. Lastly, a lawyer or any other professional acting as trustee for a foreign-law trust would fall within the scope of Moroccan anti-money laundering legislation, since all professionals will be caught by the broad scope of AML coverage. Under Article 3 of the Anti-Money Laundering Act, persons governed by the provisions of the Act are required to gather all the necessary

information to ascertain and verify the identity of their regular or occasional customers and of beneficial owners.

166. The Act applies to lawyers, notaries, auditors, external accountants and tax advisers as well as banks, financial holding companies, financial asset management companies and service providers involved in the creation, organisation and domiciliation of enterprises. Pursuant to Article 7, persons governed by the provisions of the Act must keep documents relating to the identity of their regular or occasional customers for ten years as of the date on which they close their account or cease to have relations with them.

167. In conclusion, anyone acting as a professional trustee in Morocco is required to identify his clients (settlors or beneficiaries) under AML/CTF legislation. In addition, commercial and tax obligations make it possible to identify people acting as a trustee on a professional basis and, to a certain extent, to obtain information on the settlors and beneficiaries, because otherwise the trustee will be considered as the owner of the assets of the trust and will be taxed on all the income it generates. Persons who act as a trustee on a non-professional basis are not covered by either the AML/CTF obligations or by commercial and tax obligations.

168. In practice, the Moroccan authorities and the professional representatives met during the onsite visit declared that they had never come across the case where a Moroccan resident administered a foreign trust, or where Moroccan assets were placed in trust. The probability of such a situation arising in Morocco seems low. The commercial and tax mechanisms in place nevertheless allow the settlor and beneficiaries of a trust to be identified to a certain extent, as well as the assets placed in trust and the income they generate. Lastly, no comments from peers suggested that foreign trusts were being administered by Moroccan trustees. No EOI request relating to a trust was received by Morocco during the review period.

Foundations *(ToR A.1.5)*

169. The notion of foundation is not defined in Moroccan law. However, associations exist which call themselves "foundations". They are governed by the provisions of Dahir 1-58-376 of 15 November 1958 regulating the right of association, as amended and supplemented. Article 1 of the Dahir defines an association as "the agreement by which two or more persons pool their knowledge or activity for a purpose other than to share the profits".

170. Entities also exist, created by specific statutes and calling themselves "foundations", which have a charitable, scientific, cultural, literary, sporting education, educational or healthcare purpose.

171. Article 5 of the above-mentioned Dahir states that associations must file a declaration at the headquarters of the competent local administrative authority containing:

- the association's name and purpose;
- the name, first name, nationality, age, date and place of birth, profession and domicile of the officers of the association;
- the officers' capacity to represent the association under whatever name;
- copies of their national identity card or, for foreigners, their residence permit and copies of their criminal record.

172. The articles of association must be attached to the declaration. One copy of the declaration will be filed with the prosecution service and five copies at the headquarters of the local administrative authority, which will transmit three of them to the Council Presidency (government general secretariat).

173. Any change in the administration or management of the association and any amendment of the articles of association must be declared under the same conditions with one month. Such amendments may be relied on against third parties only as of the day on which they are declared (Article 5). The administration of an association, acquisition of assets for valuable consideration or taking legal action in non-compliance with the formalities described above, is liable to a fine of MAD 1 200 to 5 000 (EUR 108 to 452) and twice that amount for a repeat offence (Article 8 of Dahir 1-58-376 of 15 November 1958 regulating the right of association). Maintaining the status of an association or the illegal restoration of the association following a judicial dissolution is liable to an imprisonment of one to six months and a fine of MAD 10 000 to 20 000 (EUR 903 to 1 800) or only one of the two sanctions (Article 8).

174. Foundations are notionally liable to corporate tax but are exempt under Article 6-I-A of the Moroccan Tax Code. They are therefore required to file a declaration of existence in the same way as companies and partnerships (Article 148 of the Moroccan Tax Code). Under Article 20, they are also subject to the same declaration requirements because they are treated as companies for the purposes of tax law (Article 2-III).

In practice

175. Monitoring and supervision of associations, including those calling themselves foundations, is the joint responsibility of the local administrative authority (the Governor or Wali) and by the associations directorate of the government general secretariat (*Direction des association du Secrétariat Général du Gouvernement* (SGG)).

176. The local administrative authority, with whom the association must be registered, performs desk-based inspections on the declaration and documents that must be produced by the association. It also verifies renewal requests from associations, following changes in their board of directors or articles of association. This administrative monitoring involves verifying the coherence of the statutory provisions and their conformity with the legislation in force, including the non-profit making nature of the activity, the compliance of the list of members of the association or the foundation with the statutory provisions and the keeping of minutes in compliance with the legislation in force (respect of the quorum, agenda, etc.). The authority also carries out onsite inspections of associations and foundations in order to ensure that the applicable regulations are being respected, including the respect of their stated purpose.

177. The associations' directorate of the SGG is in charge of ensuring the legislation and regulations governing associations and foundations are respected. To achieve this, it receives from the local administrative authorities, the registration documents of the associations or any requests for renewal, as well as a copy of all the supporting documentation (articles of association, certificate of registration, list of members of the executive board of the association, etc.). In a preliminary step, it registers the associations in a register of associations, which is a physical book that contains the name and location of the association. Then, the information provided by the local authority is entered in a database which contains the following information: the registration number, the name of the association, the Prefecture or Province in which it was formed, the type of association, the date of registration and where the physical documentation is held.

178. Should the documents or the information provided fail to comply with Moroccan legislation, the association is required by the administrative authority to provide the missing documents or make the necessary changes. The administrative authority does not have the power to automatically dissolve associations that fail to meet their legal obligations, including those with an activity that differs from that stated in the articles of association. However, the administrative authority can ask the judicial authority, namely the Tribunal of First Instance, to proceed with the legal dissolution of an association or a foundation which, for example, is carrying out a profit-making activity.

179. For each association or foundation, the existence of a physical file containing the founding documents, any requests for renewal, copies of required supporting documentation (articles of association, identity documents, etc.), means that it is possible to follow an association from its creation to its dissolution. This physical file is retained indefinitely, including after the dissolution of the association. The Associations Directorate thus holds physical files of all associations founded since 1918.

180. A national system of information on associations and foundations is being developed. All the data collected from the creation to the dissolution of the association, including information relating to the directors of the association (first and last name, date of birth, address, nationality, identity document number, etc.) will thus be available in this information system. As a result, all the data in the physical file, which will continue to be archived indefinitely, will be dematerialised, thus making the search for information easier.

181. The table below shows the number of creations and renewal of associations, including those calling themselves foundations, during the review period.

	2012	2013	2014
Number of associations registered per year	1 998	2 918	3 992
(including those calling themselves foundations)	(1)	(5)	(14)
Number of associations renewed per year	7 668	1 297	6 082
(including those calling themselves foundations)	(12)	(5)	(14)

Conclusion

182. Given the non-profit nature of Moroccan associations calling themselves “foundations” and the prior declaration and tax obligations they are required to fulfil, Moroccan law and its application in practice ensures that information about their founders and the members of their board is kept.

Enforcement provisions to ensure the availability of information (ToR A.1.6)

183. Morocco needs measure to effectively enforce provisions relating to the identification of the owners of relevant entities, including a power of access to information (see Part B below). This section of the report assesses whether penalties are applicable in the event of non-compliance with legal rules relating to identification of the owners of relevant entities.

Penalties for failure to incorporate, register or maintain information

184. All natural and legal persons, Moroccan or foreign, carrying on a commercial activity in Morocco are required to register in the commercial register. Article 62 of the Commercial Code states that any trader, manager or member of the managing bodies of a commercial company or any director of a branch or agency of an establishment or commercial company who is required by law to register in the commercial register and has failed to do so within the stipulated time is liable, on expiry of a period of one month as of service of official notice[7] by the administration, to a fine of MAD 1 000

7. Service of notice is provided for at Article 6 of decree no. 2-96-906.

to 5 000 (EUR 90 to 452). Article 63 of the Commercial Code states that the magistrate in charge of monitoring the commercial register may instruct the Commercial Court to impose that fine and order the trader in question to register within two months or be subject to a further fine.

185. Under Article 64 of the Commercial Code, the deliberate provision of inaccurate information for the purposes of registration in the commercial register is punishable by imprisonment for one month to one year and a fine of MAD 1 000 to 5 000 (EUR 90 to 452) or one only of those penalties.

186. Article 108 of Act 5-96 on partnerships, limited liability companies and joint ventures states that senior managers who fail on one or more occasions to file documents or deeds with the court registry or to carry out one or more of the publication formalities provided by law are liable to a fine of MAD 10 000 to 50 000 (EUR 903 to 4 500).

187. Under Article 245 of the law on limited companies, all subscriptions and transfers of each category of registered shares must be entered in chronological order in a register which all limited companies must keep at their registered office. This provision also applies to simplified limited companies by the application of Article 245. However, there is no penalty under Moroccan for non-compliance.

188. The administration of an association which fails to comply with the rules on prior declaration and the declaration of amendments set forth at Article 5 of Dahir 1-58-376 of 15 November 1958 regulating the right of association, is liable to a fine of MAD 1 200 to 5 000 (EUR 108 to 452) and twice that amount for a repeat offence. Maintaining the status of an association or the illegal restoration of the association following a judicial dissolution is liable to an imprisonment of one to six months and a fine of MAD 10 000 to 20 000 (EUR 903 to 1 800) or only one of the two sanctions (Article 8).

Tax legislation

189. Non-compliance with the obligation on all taxpayers, taxable or exempt, Moroccan or non-resident, to file a declaration of existence within the given time is punishable by a fine of MAD 1 000 (EUR 90). Under Article 184 of the Moroccan Tax Code, filing an inaccurate declaration is punishable by the same penalty (Article 188).

190. A discretionary tax assessment may be made in the event of failure to file a tax return or filing an incomplete or insufficient return. A 15% surcharge is applied to the discretionary assessment for failing to file the tax return (on the amount of the discretionary assessment) or filing it late (Article 184 of the Moroccan Tax Code).

191. Partnerships liable to income tax (partnerships constituted in Morocco whose partners are natural persons only and which have never opted for corporate tax) must submit an annual declaration of total income to the tax authorities (Article 82 of the Moroccan Tax Code). In addition, if the principal partner of a partnership liable to income tax (and not corporate tax) is a non-resident of Morocco, he or she must file an annual tax return in Morocco and state his or her income from Moroccan sources, including income from the partnership (Articles 23-I, 25 and 82). The penalty for failing to file tax returns or filing them late is a 15% increase in the tax levied on the profits or, if no tax return is filed, the discretionary assessment of tax (Article 184 of the Moroccan tax Code). There is no provision in the Moroccan Commercial Code for penalties for non-compliance with the accounting rules set forth at Article 19 thereof or the requirement to keep correspondence set forth at Article 26 thereof. However, deficient accounting may entail non-certification of the accounts by the statutory auditor, and under Article 231 of the Moroccan Tax Code the tax authorities may reject any accounts not kept in accordance with the prevailing accounting standards.

192. For property investment companies, failure to produce a list naming all their shareholders within the given time limit and at the same time as their tax return is punishable by a fine of MAD 10 000 (EUR 903). If the list contains omissions or errors, a fine of MAD 200 (EUR 18) is imposed for each one; however, the fine may not exceed MAD 5 000 (EUR 452) (Article 199 of the Moroccan Tax Code).

193. The penalty for failing to comply with the registration formalities and pay the duties applicable to verbal or written agreements, in the form of private or notarial deeds, relating to transfers *inter vivo*, free of charge or for valuable consideration, such as the sale, gift or exchange of shares in economic interest groupings, shares in companies not listed on a stock exchange and shares in property companies or property investment companies is set forth at Articles 184 and 208 of the Moroccan Tax Code. The penalty for non-compliance or late compliance is a 15% increase in the duties payable (Article 184) and a penalty of 10% (and an increase of 5% for the first month and 0.5% per month or part of a month thereafter) for late payment of registration duties. The sanctions applied to the failure to register transfer of shares were in 2013 and 2014 the following:

	2013	2014
Number of sanctions	1 875	1 320
Amount of sanctions (MAD)	2 545 473.04	4 324 160.37

194. In practice, the Moroccan tax administration has very dissuasive sanction at its disposal for companies that carry out their activities without

being registered with them. Firstly, any invoice issued by a company that does not have both a TIN and an ICE is non-deductible in application of Articles 11 and 145 of the Moroccan Tax Code. Thus taxpayers ensure to have commercial relations with suppliers that have a TIN and an ICE, so that not to bear non tax-deductible expenses. In addition, companies wishing to bid for public contracts must provide a certificate of compliance with their tax obligations, obtained from the tax administration.

195. Furthermore, all the tax inspection departments regularly carry out desk-based inspections using the information contained within a taxpayer's physical file and in the SIT. During this process, tax inspectors verify the compliance of tax returns with the applicable legislation (compliance checking). They also verify the information relating to the tax base, collection and payment of the tax (formal inspection). Lastly, they cross-check tax declarations with any internal and external information available to the tax administration (coherence checking). The desk-based inspection makes it possible to remind taxpayers who have failed to file a tax declaration and, where necessary, to organise onsite inspections or discretionary assessment as authorised under Moroccan law (see A2). Desk-based inspections are an effective tool that allows any inconsistency in the tax file to be identified, such as the failure to file a tax return for a given period. The Moroccan tax authorities have indicated that their target is to carry out a desk-based inspection on each taxpayer at least once every four years. The tables below show the number of desk-based inspections carried out and their results during the review period.

- In terms of direct taxation and VAT

	2012	2013	2014
Number of desk-based inspections carried out	111 200	119 322	114 782
Amount of tax recovered in MAD	2 740 160 510	3 280 316 181	1 562 155 269

- In terms of property tax and registration fees:

Number of desk-based inspections carried out	46 893	37 386	32 463
Amount of tax recovered in MAD	4 149 102 217	3 075 479 486	2 339 957 676

Anti-money laundering legislation

196. Under Article 28 of the Anti-Money Laundering Act, persons governed by the provisions of the Act and, where applicable, their managers and agents who fail to comply with the requirements set forth at Articles 3 to 9 are liable to a fine of MAD 100 000 to 500 000 (EUR 9 000 to 45 000). Criminal penalties may also apply.[8]

8. Articles 574-1 to 574-7 of the Penal Code.

Conclusion

197. Generally speaking, the penalties in force in Morocco to ensure the availability of information on ownership seem sufficiently dissuasive to ensure compliance with the statutory requirements. However, there are no penalties to enforce the obligation for limited companies, to maintain a share register (Article 254 of the law on limited companies) and the obligation, for companies, to file and keep, for 10 years, the originals of correspondence received and copies of correspondence sent (Article 26 of the Commercial Code). It is recommended that Morocco ensures that penalties for non-compliance with legal provisions relating to the identification of the owners of relevant entities exist under all circumstances.

Conclusion and factors underlying the recommendations

Phase 1 determination	
The element is in place but certain aspects of the legal implementation of the element needs improvement	
Factors underlying the recommendations	**Recommendations**
Only limited companies and partnerships limited by shares can legally issue bearer shares in Morocco, which represents less than 9% of companies with share capital. Of these, only those that expressly included this possibility in their articles of association can issue such shares. The examination by the Moroccan authorities of the articles of association of all limited companies and partnerships limited by shares did not identify any companies that had included this option in their articles of association. Although a review of corporate records did not reveal that any bearer shares had been issued or were in circulation in Morocco, Morocco still allows limited companies and limited partners of partnerships limited by shares to issue them without having introduced arrangements whereby their holders can be identified under all circumstances.	Morocco should take the necessary measures to ensure that appropriate arrangements are in place such that the holders of bearer shares can be identified under all circumstances.

Phase 1 determination	
The element is in place but certain aspects of the legal implementation of the element needs improvement	
Factors underlying the recommendations	**Recommendations**
There are no penalties to enforce the obligation for limited companies, which represent less than 9% of companies with share capital in Morocco, to maintain a share register and the obligation, for companies, to file and keep the originals of correspondence received and copies of correspondence sent.	Morocco should ensure that penalties exist in all cases for non-compliance with legal provisions relating to the identification of the owners of relevant entities.

Phase 2 rating
Partially compliant

A.2. Accounting records

Jurisdictions should ensure that reliable accounting records are kept for all relevant entities and arrangements.

198. Jurisdictions should ensure that reliable accounting records are kept for all relevant entities. Accounting records must *(i)* correctly record all transactions, *(ii)* be such that the financial situation of the entity or arrangement may be determined with reasonable precision at any time, and *(iii)* enable the preparation of financial statements. Accounting records must also be supported by underlying documentation, such as invoices, contracts, etc., and be retained for at least five years. The sources of Moroccan accounting law are Act 9-88 on accounting requirements for traders, the Commercial Code and the Moroccan Tax Code.

General requirements (ToR A.2.1)

Accounting law requirements

199. Under Act 9-88 on accounting requirements for traders (the Accounting Requirements Act), any natural or legal person having trader status within the meaning of the Commercial Code is required to keep accounts in the forms laid down by law. The requirements are general in scope and apply to all entities having trader status, whatever the status of their owners (resident or non-resident) and whatever the nature of the activity (industrial or commercial).

The accounting system must cover all operations, in chronological order, day by day, for assets and liabilities. Each record must state the origin, content and account assignment of a movement, plus the references of the supporting document (Article 1).

200. All accounts are kept by means of a system of books and accounts in compliance with the customary rules of double-entry accounting (Article 2). An inventory of the value of the enterprise's assets and liabilities must be drawn up at least once a year (Article 5).

201. Enterprises[9] must prepare annual financial statements at the end of the business year. They include the balance sheet, profits and losses statement, cashflow statement, statement of changes in financial position and notes to the accounts. They form an inseparable unit (Article 9).

202. The balance sheet separately describes the enterprise's assets and liabilities. The profits and losses statement summarises the income and expenses for the year, without giving consideration to the date of receipt or payment. The cashflow statement describes how the net profit or loss was formed and the flow of cash through the enterprise. The statement of changes in financial position shows how the enterprise's financial situation changed during the year, describing the resources available to it and how they were used. The notes supplement and comment on the information provided in the balance sheet, profits and losses statement, cashflow statement and statement of changes in financial position (Article 10). According to Article 11, the financial statements must give a true and fair view of the enterprise's assets and liabilities, financial situation and results.

203. Article 22 states that accounting records and supporting documents must be kept for ten years. The Act makes no provision for penalties for non-compliance. However, failure to keep accounting records and supporting documents may entail the loss of certain tax deductions and VAT credits. It may also entail rejection of the accounts and discretionary assessment of the taxable base for periods not time-barred.

9. Persons governed by the Accounting Requirements Act whose annual sales are less than MAD 10 million (EUR 902 000) are exempt from the requirement to prepare a cashflow statement, statement of changes in financial position or notes to the accounts (Article 21). If, due to situations specific to the enterprise, the application of an accounting rule does not give a true and fair view of the enterprise's assets and liabilities, financial situation or results, an exception may made. If that is the case, the exception is mentioned in the notes to the financial statements, stating the reasons (Article 19). Enterprises may also derogate from the rules of the Accounting Requirements Act if some or all of their operations are discontinued (Article 20).

204. The Commercial Code also contains accounting requirements. Article 19 states that traders must keep accounts in compliance with the provisions of the Accounting Requirements Act. The Commercial Code makes no provision for penalties for non-compliance. However, failure to keep accounting records and supporting documents may entail the loss of certain tax deductions and VAT credits. It may also entail rejection of the accounts and discretionary assessment of the taxable base for periods not time-barred.

205. Partnerships and professionals acting as trustees of foreign trusts are required, as traders, to comply with the above-mentioned requirements of Moroccan accounting law.

Tax law requirements

206. The Moroccan Tax Code also contains accounting requirements. Article 145 extends the obligations under the Accounting Requirements Act to all taxpayers, even if they do not have trader status, if they are liable to corporate tax, income tax on professional or farm income or VAT.

207. Under Article 145, taxpayers are required, at the end of each accounting period, to draw up detailed inventories of stocks, a list of third-party debtors and creditors including the nature, reference and detailed amount of receivables and payables, and keep a register of depreciable assets.

208. Taxpayers who are self-employed or carry on their business in the framework of a de facto partnership may, under certain conditions, opt for one of the following three schemes: simplified net profit (with simplified account-keeping requirements under Articles 38, 39 and 145 VI of the Moroccan Tax Code), lump-sum profit (Article 40) or self-employment (Article 42bis and 42ter)[10]. The simplified net profit scheme applies to taxpayers in commercial, industrial, craft or fishing professions with annual sales of less than MAD 2 million (EUR 181 000) and taxpayers who are service providers or professionals with annual sales of less than MAD 500 000 (EUR 45 000).

209. The lump-sum profit scheme applies to taxpayers in commercial, industrial, craft or fishing professions with annual sales of less than MAD 1 million (EUR 90 500) and taxpayers who are service providers with annual sales of less than MAD 250 000 (EUR 22 500). Taxpayers engaged in a regulated profession or activity are excluded from the lump-sum profit scheme.

10. Taxpayers that have opt for one of the three schemes must keep underlying documents of the purchases (article 6 of the finance law 2015, modifying the Moroccan Tax Code, law no. 100-14). Nevertheless, as traders, they are subject to accounting obligations of the Commercial Code, as described above.

210. The self-employment scheme applies to taxpayers in commercial, industrial, craft or fishing professions with annual sales of less than MAD 500 000 (EUR 22 500) and to service providers with annual sales of less than MAD 200 000 (EUR 18 000).

211. Article 147 of the Moroccan Tax Code states that non-resident enterprises which have a permanent activity in Morocco must keep the accounts of all the transactions they carry out in Morocco at the place where they have their main place of business, in compliance with Moroccan law. Non-resident companies that have opted for flat-rate corporate tax must keep a register of payments received and transfers, a register of salaries paid to Moroccan and foreign employees, including the related social security contributions, and a register of fees, commission, brokerage fees and other similar remuneration paid to third parties in Morocco or abroad. Under Article 1 of the Accounting Requirements Act, if non-resident companies are trading companies or if their transactions are liable to VAT, they must also comply with the provisions of the Act.

212. The financial statements constitute accounting and tax packages which must be produced within three months of the end of the business year. They must be filed with the commercial register for public information purposes and with the tax authorities for taxation purposes.

213. Article 20 of the Moroccan Tax Code states that the tax return must include annexes, a list of which is drawn up by regulation. Finance Ministry order no. 297-88 of 6 rejeb 1408 (24 February 1988) on the annexes that companies are required to provide to the administration in support of their tax return states that the following documents must be submitted to the tax authorities:

- the balance sheet showing assets and liabilities;
- a table of earnings including profits and losses;
- a statement of non-accounting adjustments;
- a statement of sales giving a breakdown between domestic and export sales;
- a detailed statement of inventories;
- a statement of overheads;
- a table of fixed assets and depreciations;
- a statement of depreciation and amortisation expense;
- a statement of provisions;
- a statement of interest on loans;

- a statement of capital gains from mergers;
- a statement of transferable securities;
- a statement of leases;
- a statement of shareholdings;
- a statement of allocation of earnings.

214. Article 145 of the Moroccan Tax Code extends the provisions of the Accounting Requirements Act to all taxpayers liable to tax, even if they do not have trader status. The accounting requirements arising from tax law also apply to partnerships and professionals acting as trustees for a foreign trust. Foundations, which have the legal form of associations, are also subject to the accounting rules set forth at Articles 145 to 147 of the Moroccan Tax Code, because under Article 2-III of the Code they are treated as companies for the purposes of its application.

215. Under Article 211 of the Moroccan Tax Code, taxpayers are required to keep the necessary documents for a tax audit for ten years at the place where they are taxed. The penalties for non-compliance with the requirement relating to how the accounting records must be kept set forth at Articles 145 and 146 of the Moroccan Tax Code are set forth at Article 191 of the Code. Article 191 of the Moroccan Tax Code sets out the penalties for failure to comply with requirements to keep accounting records: MAD 2 000 (EUR 180) for each day's delay and a daily fine of MAD 100 (EUR 9) up to a limit of MAD 1 000 (EUR 90) for taxpayers who fail to present the accounting records and supporting documents referred to at Articles 145 and 146 of the Moroccan Tax Code. However, there is no penalty for failing to keep records for the ten-year period stipulated at Article 211. However, failure to keep accounting records and supporting documents may entail the loss of certain tax deductions and VAT credits. It may also entail rejection of the accounts and discretionary assessment of tax for periods not time-barred.

216. In addition, the sanction for failure or lateness in filing a tax return and providing tax and accounting documentation is a 15% surcharge on the amount of tax payable (Article 184 of the Moroccan Tax Code). A penalty of 5% for the first late month, followed by 0.5% per month for each additional month or part of month is also payable in case of late payment of the tax. A 1% surcharge is applied for failing to make an online declaration and a 1% surcharge is also applied for failing to make an online payment of the tax (Article 187 bis and 208 bis CGI).

217. Offshore banks, in addition to complying with the legal, accounting and tax requirements described above, must also submit their financial statements together with an external auditors' report to the committee responsible for offshore banks (Article 125 of the law on offshore financial centres,). The

committee comprises a representative of the finance ministry, a representative of the central bank and a representative of the foreign exchange office (Article 23 of the law on offshore financial centres). The penalty for failure to comply with this requirement is loss of offshore bank status. Offshore companies, whether banks or holding companies, are liable to the same legal and tax requirements with regard to accounting than any other entities.

In practice

218. As with registration and amended registrations, traders must submit their financial statements each year to the clerk of the competent court (Commercial Court, or Court of First Instance if there is no Commercial Court). These financial statements are recorded by the clerk and retained indefinitely. As explained in the examination of element A.1., supervision of the commercial register is the responsibility of the Secretary Clerk under the control of the President of the Court, or a judge designated by him. The latter is in charge of sending copies of the financial statements to the OMPIC which then centralises them at the national level and publishes them online via their web portal www.directinfo.ma. During the review period, the number of financial statements registered by OMPIC was 110 806 in 2012, 123 306 in 2013 and 133 858 in 2014 respectively.

219. The tax authorities also hold accounting information about taxpayers. The tax authorities are in charge of ensuring that accounting obligations are respected by all taxpayers, whether they are natural or legal persons, partnerships or companies with share capital, foreign companies or Moroccan companies. This supervision takes the form of monitoring annual tax returns and the accompanying tax and accounting documentation, and also by auditing these declarations.

220. Registered companies have three months from the close of the financial year to file a tax return which must be accompanied by the supporting accounting and tax information and the list of the 10 principal partners or shareholders. Should there be a failure to file the tax return or any supporting documentation, or should the file be incomplete, the tax authorities will enforce the measures of Article 228 of the Moroccan Tax Code. The tax authorities notify the taxpayer by registered mail, or by letter handed to him by a sworn tax official, a bailiff, a clerk of the court, requiring all outstanding obligations to be met within 30 days following reception of the notice. If the taxpayer continues to fail to meet these obligations within this timeframe, the same tax department will send a registered letter informing the taxpayer of the discretionary assessment basis on which they will be taxed if the tax return or missing documents are not filed within 30 days of receiving this new letter. If the taxpayer continues to fail to respond to these requests, then taxpayer will be taxed based on this discretionary assessment.

The table below shows the level of compliance of the taxpayer with their tax obligations:

	Number of taxpayers (1)	Taxpayers having filed their tax return (2)	Compliance rate (2)/(1)
2012	763 499	639 919	83.81%
2013	817 578	653 211	79.90%
2014	869 561	605 654	69.65%

221. The sanctions available under Moroccan law for failure to file a tax return, filing an incomplete tax return or the late filing of a tax return and the required supporting documentation, as well as in the case of a discretionary assessment, are applied in practice, as the table below shows.

	2012	2013	2014
Surcharges	MAD 1 398 371 198	MAD 2 039 020 725	MAD 1 195 272 433
Penalties	MAD 609 033 929	MAD 689 983 005	MAD 721 066 434
Surcharges for late filing	MAD 1 907 102 407	MAD 2 411 393 896	MAD 1 971 930 327
Fines	MAD 73 132 098	MAD 121 053 538	MAD 99 082 275
Total	MAD 3 987 639 632	MAD 5 261 451 163	MAD 3 987 351 469

222. The tax administration also carries out checks to ensure the availability of accounting information. As indicated in the review of element A.1, the tax administration performs desk-based inspections (compliance, form and coherence checks) of taxpayer tax returns. The tax administration can require the taxpayer to present any documentation that is required by law to be retained. Thus, the tax administration carried out 111 200 desk-based inspections on taxable income and VAT declarations by taxpayers in 2012, 119 322 in 2013 and 114 782 in 2014. The tax administration also verifies that taxpayers are respecting their accounting obligations, using onsite tax audits. Within the context of these operations, the tax inspectors are shown all documents required by the law to be retained, in particular accounting records and supporting documentation. If there are serious irregularities in the accounting, it can be rejected, and the tax inspectors will use the information at their disposal to recalculate the turnover, on which the tax will be based.

223. Lastly, the tax administration also makes effective use of its right of inspection, pursuant to Article 210 of the Moroccan Tax Code. The aim of the right of inspection is to allow the tax administration to make unannounced spot-checks in a company, in order to ensure that invoicing rules and accounting procedures are being scrupulously respected. This procedure, which starts when the investigation notice is served, can last up to eight days. The

tax inspectors will examine all documents relating to operations that have or should have been included in an invoice, will verify that the accounting records exist and will make a material observation of the operating assets in order to look for potential deficiencies. At the end of the procedure a concluding report is prepared. The observation included in this report can then be used against the taxpayer in the case of a tax audit.

224. The table below illustrates the use of onsite tax audits and right of inspection by the tax administration during the review period.

	2012	2013	2014
Number of onsite audits carried out	1 774	1 415	1 439
Number of rights of inspection carried out	3	16	7

Conclusion

225. In view of both its accounting and its tax legislation, Morocco ensures the availability of accounting information from which it is possible to accurately trace all transactions, assess the financial position of all relevant entities and prepare financial statements for them.

226. In practice, there is effective monitoring of the obligation to file a tax return as well as the supporting accounting and tax documentation and the list of the ten principal partners or shareholders. This information is integrated into the SIT system, which makes it directly available to the tax authorities. The tax authorities have the right to send reminders for non-compliance and can apply dissuasive sanctions when the accounting information is not filed or is incomplete. It also performs regular desk inspections of taxpayers, can carry out onsite audits to check accounting information and can use its right of inspection.

227. During the review period, Morocco received 61 EOI requests for accounting information, including supporting documentation. In their commentaries, the peers indicated that when responses were received from Morocco they were satisfactory. However, around 15 EOI requests for accounting information from Morocco's partners did not receive a response during the review period. Given the mechanisms for ensuring the availability of accounting information in Morocco as well as their effective supervision, the review team believes that this situation can be explained by the EOI organisation and processes in Morocco during the review period (see C.5).

Underlying documentation (ToR A.2.2)

228. Under Moroccan accounting law, each record must state the origin, content and charging of the movement, plus the references of the underlying document (Article 1 of the Accounting Requirements Act).

229. Tax law also refers to underlying documents. All purchases of goods or services made by a taxpayer from a supplier liable to business tax must be justified by a proper invoice or any other documentary evidence made out in the name of the interested party. In addition to the customary commercial information, the invoice or document in lieu must include the seller's identity, the tax identification number (TIN), the date of the transaction, the name and first name or company name and address of the buyers or customers, the price, quantity and nature of the goods sold, work performed or services rendered, the amount of VAT, the method of payment and all other information required by the prevailing laws and regulations (Articles 145 and 146).

230. In addition, Article 210 of the Moroccan Tax Code on the tax administration's right of audit states that taxpayers, whether natural or legal persons, must provide all justifications, including accounting records and underlying documents. Article 211 states that underlying documents for current and capital expenditure must also be kept such as "copies of sale invoices or till receipts, supporting documents for current and capital expenditure and the necessary accounting records for tax audit purposes, including in particular the books in which the transactions were recorded, the general ledger, the inventory ledger, detailed inventories, the day-book, customer and supplier factsheets and any other document required by tax law".

231. In practice, the tax administrations ensures that taxpayers retain the appropriate supporting documents for their accounts (invoices, delivery notes, etc.) when carrying out desk-based inspections, and onsite audits. If these supporting documents are absent, or if the invoicing rules are not respected, expenses and VAT will not be tax deductible. They can also represent a serious accounting irregularity that could lead to the rejection of the taxpayers' accounting records and the recalculation of the turnover by the tax administration. The use of the right of inspection also makes it possible to check whether invoicing rules are being respected and ensure that invoices and other supporting documents exist and are being retained.

Document retention (ToR A.2.3)

232. Accounting records and supporting documents must be kept for ten years pursuant to Article 22 of the Accounting Requirement Act.

233. The Moroccan Tax Code states that taxpayers and natural or legal persons required to withhold tax at source are required to keep, for ten years

at the place where they are taxed, copies of sale invoices or till receipts, underlying documents for expenses and investments and the necessary accounting records for tax audit purposes, including in particular the books in which the transactions were recorded, the general ledger, the inventory ledger, detailed inventories and any other document required by tax law (Article 211).

234. Moreover, the persons subject to the AML/CTF law must retain all documents relating to the operations carried out by their clients for ten years from the date of the action (Article 7 of the anti-money laundering law).

235. Having regard to the tax and accounting requirements set out in the various laws in force in Morocco, the requirement to retain accounting records for at least five years exists.

236. Moroccan commercial and tax law does not include any direct sanction for failing to keep accounting records and supporting documentation for ten years. Article 28 of the anti-money laundering law states that failure by persons subject to the obligation to keep records of documents relating to operations carried out by their clients can be sanctioned by a fine of between MAD 100 000 and MAD 500 000 (EUR 9 000 to EUR 45 000). However, this sanction does not ensure that accounting records and supporting documents will be retained in all cases by all taxpayers.

237. Indirect sanctions do exist, such as for example the refusal to allow charges to be tax deducted or the rejection of the accounting records. Having said this, the implementation of indirect sanctions is limited by the four year limitation period included in Article 232 of the Moroccan Tax Code. Indeed, inadequacies, errors or omissions observed in the determination of the tax base and the calculation of the tax, or the filling of a tax return on time can only be sanctioned until 31 December of the fourth year following the tax year in question. Consequently, the tax administration cannot apply tax sanctions for failure to keep records on a time-barred tax year. However, the limitation period can be extended in some specific circumstances. For instance, when a VAT deficit or credit is carried over from a time-barred tax year to one that is still applicable, the tax administration can extend its tax audit to the closer four time-bared tax years. Other than this situation where the tax administration can audit up to eight tax years, the tax administration can apply no tax consequences for accounting failures (failure to keep accounts, irregular accounting, absence of supporting documentation, etc.) in a time-barred tax year. Consequently, Moroccan legislation does not ensure that accounting records and supporting documentation is conserved for at least five years in all circumstances.

238. The finances law no. 70-15 for the 2016 budget year has added to point VIII of Article 232 of the Moroccan Tax Code a new provision under which the tax due as well as the penalties and relevant surcharges that are applicable

to taxpayers who have failed to file a tax declaration are payable in full for all the years where a tax declaration was not filed, even if these years are now time-barred, to a limit of 10 years. Therefore this change to the law, which occurred outside of the review period, allows the tax administration to draw tax consequences in the event of failure to keep accounting records and supporting documentation in a time-barred tax year. However, this measure is limited to the hypothesis of a failure to file a tax return. It does not allow, for example, sanctioning a taxpayer who is no longer in possession of accounting records and supporting documentation for a time-barred tax year where a tax declaration has been filed, even if this tax declaration is incomplete.

239. In conclusion, although Moroccan law requires taxpayers and traders to keep accounting records and supporting documentation for 10 years, this obligation is accompanied by no direct sanction. Although dissuasive tax sanctions can be applied for failure to comply with the record-keeping obligation, the application of these sanctions is not guaranteed beyond the four year limitation period. Morocco is therefore recommended to ensure that appropriate sanctions are applicable in all cases of failure to keep accounting records and supporting documentation for a minimum period of five years.

240. In practice, as explained above, the tax authorities carries out effective monitoring of the declarative obligation of taxpayers, using the powers available under Moroccan law.

Conclusion and factors underlying the recommendations

Phase 1 determination	
The element is in place but certain aspects of the legal implementation needs improvement.	
Factors underlying the recommendations	**Recommendations**
According to Moroccan laws, accounting records and supporting documentation must be kept for 10 years. However, there is no direct sanction for failure to respect this obligation, although dissuasive tax sanctions can be applied in this case. However, given the time-bar rules, the sanction for failure to keep accounting records or supporting documents beyond the four years of the time-bar is not guaranteed in certain situations.	Morocco must ensure that appropriate sanctions are applicable in all cases for non-compliance with the requirement to keep accounting records including supporting documentation for at least five years.

Phase 2 rating
Largely compliant.

A.3. Banking information

Banking information should be available for all account-holders.

241. Access to banking information is of interest to the tax authorities only if the bank has useful and reliable information on its customers' identity and the nature and amount of financial transactions.

Record-keeping requirements (ToR A.3.1)

242. Banks, credit institutions and similar organisations are governed by Morocco's anti-money laundering (AML) legislation. As mentioned in Section A.1.1, under Article 2 of the Anti-Money Laundering Act, banks are subject to its requirements. They are thus required to gather all information enabling them to verify the identity of their regular or occasional customers and of beneficial owners (Article 3).

243. Article 5 of the Act states that banks are required to regularly update their customer files. The Act does not give any definition of the term "customer". The authorities said that "customer" means any natural or legal person who receives a good or service from an enterprise. If the identity of customers and beneficial owners cannot be verified, or if it is incomplete or plainly fictitious, persons governed by the Act must not perform transactions (Article 4) or enter into or continue business relations (Article 5).

244. With regard to persons governed by the Act that are legally authorised to open accounts, they must, before opening an account, ascertain and verify the identity of the persons in favour of whom it is opened, when they consider that the persons who have asked for the account to be opened were not acting on their own behalf. In addition, they may not open anonymous accounts or accounts in fictitious names (Article 6).

245. Persons governed by the Act must keep documents relating to transactions carried out by their customers for ten years as of the execution date. They must also keep documents relating to the identity of their regular or occasional customers for ten years as of the date on which they close their account or cease to have relations with them (Article 7).

246. The supervisory authority for banks with regard to compliance with anti-money laundering requirements is the central bank, Bank Al-Maghrib.

247. Persons governed by the Act and, where applicable, their managers and agents who fail to comply with the requirements described in this section are liable to a fine of MAD 100 000 to 500 000 (EUR 9 000 to 45 000) in accordance with Article 28. Criminal or regulatory penalties may also apply in application of Article 1 of the Anti-Money Laundering Act and Book III, Title I, Chapter IX of the Penal Code approved by Dahir 1-59-413 of 28 joumada II 1382 (26 November 1962).

248. Banks and other financial institutions are subject to the same record-keeping requirements as all other trading entities and taxpayers, as stipulated in Moroccan accounting and tax law and as described in Section A.2.

249. In conclusion, with regard to banking activity, Morocco's anti-money laundering legislation ensures the availability of information about identity and ownership and of financial and accounting information for ten years.

Availability of banking information in practice

250. Correct implementation of the AML/CTF measures is a major concern of the BAM. Within the banking supervision directorate (*Direction de la supervision bancaire*) of the BAM, it is mainly two departments who are involved in the supervision and control of credit establishments, which consist of 19 banks, 6 offshore banks, 10 payment establishments (money transfers companies), 34 financing companies and 13 micro-credit associations.

251. One of the two departments is the permanent supervision department (*Département de la surveillance permanente*). It is in charge of the permanent supervision and desk-based control of credit establishments with regards to all their legal and regulatory obligations, including AML/CTF obligations. It consists of 27 officials who are assigned to the documentary control. Thus, this department assesses the AML/CTF measures of these establishments, based on their responses to an annual questionnaire. It also uses annual internal auditing and compliance reports which have to be submitted by the 31 March of the year following the previous tax year, and which contain a section on AML/CTF efforts. It also examines statutory auditors' reports as well as reports from the host countries of subsidiaries of Moroccan credit establishments abroad, within the framework of cross-border supervision. The statutory auditors as well as the bank can be required at any time to provide explanations to the permanent supervision department as part of its controls. In addition, regular meetings with these parties are organised. If there are substantial shortcomings in the desk-based inspection, an onsite inspection may be organised.

252. As part of its duties, the permanent supervision department has a system for rating credit establishments, the SANEC (*Système d'Aide de Notation des Établissements de Crédit*). This is an analysis and prevention

tool that allows risk-based supervision, and a tool for internal management that allows the intensity of permanent monitoring to be dimensioned, onsite missions to be decided and corrective measures to be taken. The SANEC system notably includes a specific criteria (criteria no. 14) dedicated to the assessment of the AML/CTF measures in place.

253. The second department is the onsite inspections department (*Département du contrôle sur place*) of the BAM, which consists of 21 officials. It carries out general or thematic inspections in credit establishments based on an annual programme that is decided upon notably by taking into account the ratings of the SANEC system, in conjunction with the financial integrity department. The general investigations assess all the activities of an establishment and systematically include a review of the AML/CTF measures. The thematic investigations examine one particular aspect of these activities, such as AML/CTF measures and can cover more than one establishment at a time. The onsite inspection complements the permanent monitoring by using targeted investigations that seek to evaluate the quality of the internal audit and risk-management measures and the governance of the credit establishments.

254. The officials from the onsite inspections department have an audit manual which defines the AML/CTF diligences to respect when onsite. In this way, the monitoring of the AML/CTF measures is a two-step process.

- The first step seeks to assess the risks, the organisation and the permanent monitoring of the activity, analysing the answers to the AML/CTF questionnaire, procedures and monitoring tools and assessing the extent of staff awareness and training;
- The second step seeks to check client and accounts files, account-opening files, and examine declarations made to UTRF. This is also when customer identification and documentation is examined along with the respect of registration, reporting and retention obligations on operations carried out on the account (opening, operations, closing).

Thus, the inspectors assess the compliance and internal audit of AML/CTF measures as well as governance of the establishment during the financial year. The table below shows the types of onsite inspection carried out by the BAM.

	2012	2013	2014	2015
General onsite inspections	2 banks	4 banks	2 banks	4 banks 2 subsidiaries of Moroccan banks in Africa 2 financing companies
Themed AML/CTF onsite inspections				1 bank

255. In 2013 and 2014, inspections carried out by BAM resulted in administrative sanctions (injunctions and warnings) being addressed to a number of establishments and financial penalties being levied on others for non-respect of various regulations. However, there was no sanction related to non-compliance with AML/CTF obligations. In 2015, one bank had financial penalties levied against it due to failure to comply with the AML/CTF legislation.

256. Since January 2016, a new department dedicated to the assessment of the financial integrity has been created. This department is in charge of:

- The assessment of the LAB/CTF framework of the credit establishment, the monitoring of the recommendations formulated following the inspections of these establishments. Where necessary, this department can also propose the application of sanctions available under Moroccan law.
- The monitoring of the relation with the UTRF, the AML/CTF practices and the relations with the competent international bodies.

257. In addition, in application of Article 160 of Law 103.12 relating to credit establishments and assimilated organisations, known as the "*loi bancaire*" (banking law) adopted in November 2014 and published in 2015, the BAM created the bank account centralisation department (SCCB, *Service de la Centralisation des Comptes Bancaires*). This department centralises all the current and deposit accounts that are opened, amended or closed by credit establishments. However, the balances are not followed up. The data registered with the SCCB is held for 10 years following the closure of the account. This service was launched on 21 December 2015 and information is provided quarterly by credit establishments. The tax authorities are currently holding discussions with BAM to determine the conditions under which the tax administration would have access to the SCCB.

258. Lastly, credit establishments are subject to the same obligations and the same controls as described in section A1 and A2 for all companies.

259. In conclusion, credit establishments in Morocco are subject to close supervision by the BAM, notably regarding the identification of their customers and the reporting and recording of bank account operations. The extent and intensity of the monitoring make banking information available in Morocco.

260. Over the review period, Morocco received 65 EOI requests for banking information (account numbers, statements, balances, etc.). In their commentary, the peers indicated that when responses were received from Morocco they were satisfactory. However, around 10 EOI requests for banking information from Morocco's partners did not receive a response during the review period. Given the mechanisms for ensuring the availability of

banking information in Morocco as well as their effective supervision, the review team believe that this situation can be explained by the way EOI organisation and processes in Morocco during the review period (see C.5).

Conclusion and factors underlying the recommendations

Phase 1 determination
The element is in place.

Phase2 rating
Compliant

B. Access to information

Overview

261. A variety of information may be needed in a tax enquiry and jurisdictions should have the authority to obtain all such information. This includes information held by banks and other financial institutions as well as information concerning the ownership of companies or identity of interest holders in other persons or entities, such as partnerships or trusts, as well as accounting information in respect of all such entities. This section of the report examines whether Morocco's legal and regulatory framework gives the authorities powers that cover all relevant persons and information and whether taxpayers' rights and safeguards are compatible with the effective exchange of information.

262. The competent authority for exchange of information requests received by Morocco is the Finance Minister, who may delegate this power to one or more persons. This power has been delegated to the Director-General of Taxes. The Moroccan authorities use the powers available to them for domestic tax matters for the purposes of international exchanges of information.

263. Under the provisions on the right to information and the right of inspection in the Moroccan Tax Code, the Moroccan tax authorities have extensive powers of access to accounting and banking information and to information on the ownership of legal entities. The tax authorities also have a power to control declarations and instruments used to determine taxes and duties.

264. With these powers, the tax authorities may, inter alia, ask any taxpayer, third party or other administration to provide appropriate information in order to assess and control taxes and duties. These collection powers, which have their origin in Moroccan domestic law, also apply to any request for information under an international convention, in accordance with the principle that international conventions take precedence over domestic law, as provided for in the Moroccan Constitution. The sanctions for failing to provide information or documents seem to be sufficiently dissuasive to ensure the Moroccan tax authorities will be able to obtain this information.

265. Professional secrecy obligations are not an obstacle to EOI, other than in the cases that are allowed by the standard.

266. Powers of access to information are backed up by measures to enforce the provision of information. Furthermore, under Article 181 of Act 103-12 on credit institutions and similar organisations, banking secrecy cannot be asserted against the tax authorities for the application of bilateral conventions on the exchange of information for tax purposes and there is no provision relating to rights and safeguards which could hamper or unduly delay an effective exchange of information.

267. During the review period, Morocco received 182 EOI requests from its partners. Morocco was able to provide information and documents of all types to its partners with regards to EOI. However, 58 EOI requests did not receive a response during the review period. The review team believe that this situation can be explained by EOI organisation and processes in Morocco during the review period. Morocco has effective powers for accessing information that are implemented in practice, and without professional secrecy obligations being used to oppose this, other than where allowed by the standard.

B.1. Competent authority's ability to obtain and provide information

Competent authorities should have the power to obtain and provide information that is the subject of a request under an exchange of information arrangement from any person within their territorial jurisdiction who is in possession or control of such information (irrespective of any legal obligation on such person to maintain the secrecy of the information).

Powers to access information under Morocco's domestic tax law

268. Morocco's competent authority for the exchange of information, as provided for by international tax conventions, is the Finance Minister or the person or persons delegated for that purpose. The persons to whom that authority has been delegated are the Director General of Taxes, the Director of Legislation, Research and International Cooperation, the Director of Tax Audits, the Head of the International Cooperation Division, the Head of the Data Consistency Division and the Head of the International Tax Conventions Department.

269. Powers to gather information for exchange purposes are based on Moroccan domestic law. They are the same powers as those the tax authorities use for their own purposes.

*Ownership and identity information (ToR **B.1.1.**)*

270. In Morocco, information from tax returns is in the possession of the tax authorities, and certain information held by Customs and Indirect Tax Authority (such as the amount of imports and exports) and the Treasury (such as the amount of public procurement contracts and detailed breakdowns).

271. Where requested information is not in the tax authorities' possession, they may assert their right to information provided for at Article 214 of the Moroccan Tax Code. The right to information applies not only to taxpayers but also to other administrations. The article states that in order to obtain any relevant information with regard to the assessment and control of taxes and duties payable by third parties, the tax authorities may ask for:

- official documents or accounting records held by government agencies, local authorities, public corporations and any organisation under state control, given that professional secrecy may not be asserted as a ground for withholding them;
- books and documents which must be kept pursuant to the prevailing laws and regulations, and all instruments, writings, registers and files held by natural or legal persons carrying on a business liable to taxes or duties.

272. Requests for information must be made in writing. Article 214 of the Moroccan Tax Code states that the right to information is exercised on the premises of the registered office or main place of business of the natural or legal persons concerned, where documents may be copied with the taxpayer's consent, unless the interested parties provide the information in writing or hand the information to tax officials in return for a receipt.

273. During the review period, no binding timeframe had been set forth in Article 214 within which a right to information notice from the tax authorities must be answered. However, Dahir n°-15-150 of the 7 rabii I 1437 (19 December 2015) enacting the finances law no. 70-15 for the 2016 financial year, included in Article 214 of the Moroccan Tax Code the obligation to respond to right to information notices from the tax administration within a maximum of 30 days following the date of reception of the aforementioned notice.

274. The right to information set forth at Article 214 also allows the tax authorities to request information from the tax authorities of countries which have concluded conventions with Morocco designed to avoid double taxation of income. The Moroccan authorities have confirmed that this right to information would also be applicable under the Multilateral Convention.

275. In addition, the tax authorities also have the power to check declarations and documents used in order to assess taxes and duties. For that purpose, taxpayers, whether natural or legal persons, are required to provide all necessary evidence and provide all accounting records to tax officials (Article 210 of the Moroccan Tax Code).

276. The tax authorities also have a right of inspection whereby they may ask taxpayers to provide invoices and books, registers and business documents relating to transactions that have given rise or should give rise to an invoice, and materially ascertain physical elements of the business in order to identify non-compliance with requirements under the prevailing laws and regulations (Article 210 of the Moroccan Tax Code). However, the Moroccan tax authorities' powers do not include a right of search or seizure.

277. Lastly, the Moroccan tax administration may, where necessary, access information by carrying out an onsite audit. Under the provisions of Article 212 of the Moroccan Tax Code, the tax administration may carry out a general audit or spot-check in the company premises. In all cases, the tax auditor has the right to access any document that is required by law to be retained, whether these are accounting documents or not. Tax audits follow a strictly-defined procedure in order to preserve the rights and guarantees of the taxpayer. The latter must be given 15 days notice in writing of the date of the inspection, as well as the taxes and the tax years being inspected. The taxpayer also has the right to be assisted by an adviser of his or her choice. Although in principle, only tax years that are not time-barred are audited, time-barred years may still be controlled if they have an impact on the non time-barred tax year (for example, the inspection of loss-making years when the loss is deducted against a non-time barred profit-making tax year, or checking a VAT credit for the time barred period, when this credit is carried forward over a non-time-barred period). While on-site tax audits may not be the most useful way of obtaining information about a taxpayer, they can be used for EOI purposes, particularly when the taxpayer targeted by an EOI request is already the subject of an on-site tax audit.

278. Exercise of the right to information and right of inspection are not limited in time or time-barred in Moroccan tax law. However, as taxpayers are required to keep accounting records and underlying documents for ten years, in practice these rights are not exercised beyond a ten-year period.

Banking information

279. The information-gathering powers described above also apply to banking information. The right to information set forth at Article 214 of the Moroccan Tax Code states that the tax authorities may request all relevant information for the assessment and control of taxes and duties payable by

third parties. Consequently, the Moroccan authorities may ask banks and other financial institutions for banking information relating to account holders or other bank customers, including offshore banks.

Accounting records (ToR B.1.2)

280. In Morocco, accounting information is available from the tax authorities because all taxpayers must file financial statements comprising accounting and tax packages with the court registry for public information purposes and with the tax authorities for taxation purposes within three months of the closing date of each accounting period (Article 158 of the law on limited companies, Article 95 of the law on partnerships, limited liability companies and joint ventures, and Articles 20 and 82 of the Moroccan Tax Code).

281. This information is also available from the competent court, the OMPIC or directly from entities themselves.

282. The conditions for access to information on ownership and identity described in Section B.1.1 above apply to accounting information in the same way, with the same possibilities for access and the same limits.

283. The tax authorities can verify accounting records by application of their right to check under Article 210 of the Moroccan Tax Code to inspect declarations and documents used in order to assess taxes and duties. For that purpose, taxpayers whether natural or legal persons, are required to provide all necessary evidence and provide all accounting records to tax officials.

Information-gathering in practice

284. During the review period, Morocco received 182 EOI requests from its partners. Of these, 78 were regarding ownership, 61 related to accounting information, and 65 related to banking information. Most of the EOI requests were seeking various categories of information. However, 58 EOI requests from Morocco's EOI partners, not specifically referring to any type of information, did not receive a response during the review period. The review team believes that this situation can be explained by EOI organisation and processes in Morocco during the review period (see C.5). In practice, the Moroccan tax administration already has access to much information in their databases and physical files, and where necessary it also uses its powers to access information.

Information available to the tax authorities

285. Within the tax administration, the Cross-Referencing and Investigation Department (SREF, *Service des recoupements et des enquêtes fiscales*) has direct access to all the information held by the DGI in its information system.

286. Thus it has full access to the SIT system which contains all the information collected during taxpayer registration, namely the information needed to identify the taxpayer and manage their tax obligations. In particular, this includes the identity information of the taxpayer (legal form, first and last names and nationality for a natural person, company name and trading name for a legal person), their identification numbers (TIN, ICE, social security number and commercial register number, land title number and business tax number), information relating to their taxation (tax regime, date and place of creation of the company, main activity and secondary activities) and the identity of the company directors (first and last name, address, telephone number, email address), their bank account details, identification of partners or shareholders (first and last name, address, identity document number, TIN, telephone and fax number, email address, whether they are the main partner or not, and for shareholders only, their profession) and lastly the contact details of the tax department in charge of their file.

287. However, the supporting documentation that has to be provided when the taxpayer is registered, such as articles of association, proof of tax residency, copies of identity documents or the proof that all the identification details of the taxpayer have been provided to the tax authorities, the commercial register and the social security are not available in the SIT system. These documents are kept indefinitely by the tax department in charge of the file in the taxpayer's hard-copy file. The SREF can have access to the hard-copy file of a taxpayer by making a request by email to the Director of the DRI. A digital copy of the requested document is sent by email to the SREF within a maximum of 30 days.

288. In addition, the SIT system is progressively integrating all the information relative to the tax base and tax collection as the system of online tax declarations and payments becomes more widespread. In 2017, it will apply to all taxpayers, but at the moment, the obligation to make an online tax declaration and payment concerns *(i)* companies with a turnover greater than or equal to MAD 10 million (EUR 900 000), not including VAT, and *(ii)* taxpayers carrying out certain liberal professions. Through the use of these online services, the SIT offers direct access to the following information:

- For companies: tax returns accompanied by the supporting documents; summary statements of payments made to third parties or non-residents; income from fixed-income investments; income from shares, capital rights and assimilated income; proceeds from the transfer of securities made in Morocco by non-resident companies, and monthly and quarterly VAT declarations.
- For individuals: the declaration of global income, declaration of payments and salaries, of payments made to non-residents, payments made to third parties, profits from securities, capital or monthly income from insurance companies, real estate profits, income from

fixed-income investments, income from shares, capital rights and assimilated income and the declaration of a change in tax domicile.

However, for companies or individuals who do not file their declaration online, the above-mentioned information is available in the physical files of the DRI department in charge of the taxpayer, and is accessible to the SREF according to the procedure described above for the documents that accompany the registration procedure.

289. In addition, the SIT system, which already contains information on the taxpayer's bank account, systematically collects new bank details used during the online payment of taxes, which enriches the banking information directly available to the tax authorities for the purposes of cross-referencing, tax collection and EOI.

290. Finally, the information collected during the registration formalities for transfer of movable and immovable assets are also directly available from the SIT system. The tax officers of the DRI in charge of registration formalities directly enter into the SIT system the information contained in the documents that have to be provided in order to proceed with the registration. In addition, in 2015 the DGI and the order of notaries signed an automatic data transmission agreement that involved linking the Tawtik system, developed by the national council of the order of notaries, with the tax administration's SIT system. Thus, the registration of notarised deeds is dematerialised and the information gathered by notaries is directly entered into the SIT system. The information that is thus directly available includes that of the department that carried out the registration and those of the person who filed the deed, and the other party to the deed (TIN, names or company names, nature of the operation, number of land deeds if it is a real estate transaction, value, form of the deed, date of filing, timeframe, registration number). However, the copy of the deed is not available in the SIT system but in the physical files maintained by the competent registry office of the DRI.

291. The SREF also has access to information from a number of different databases:

- Identification details of natural persons and their income tax returns are available via the national income tax database: name, address, TIN, tax base, amount of tax paid, etc.
- Identification details of companies and their corporate tax return are available via the national corporate tax database: company name and trading name TIN, turnover, profits, shareholders/partners, etc.);
- Addresses of people and entities can be obtained from the national housing tax database (*Fichier National de la Taxe d'Habitation*) and the customer databases of electricity and water companies.

- Patrimonial information, if it is not available from the registration process in the SIT system, can be obtained from the national housing tax database, providing the premises are subject to housing tax.
- Information on partners and shareholders (first name, last name or company name, address, shares, etc.) is available from the databases of shareholders and partners in large and medium-sized companies, a non-exhaustive list compiled by the STRF and completed by the database obtained from the OMPIC.
- Property ownership information (extracted from the property ownership deeds) proving the deed number is known, is available directly via the internet from the database of the National Land and Property Registry (*Agence Nationale du Cadastre et de la Conservation Foncière,* ANCCF). This database encompasses notably the following information: first and last names of the owner, number of the property deed, type of right, identity number, date of birth, etc.

292. Lastly, Morocco intends to dematerialise the cross-referencing management by putting in place an automatic cross-referencing system (*Système Automatisé des Recoupements*). This will enable an interconnection between the various internal and external databases to which the tax administration have access for cross-referencing purposes.

Information held by the taxpayer or a third party

293. When the required information is not already held by the tax administration, it can use the information-gathering powers accorded to them under Moroccan law. To this end, they generally use the right to information procedure to obtain from third parties the original or a digital or hard copy of the information they hold.

294. Thus, the tax administration uses their right to information to obtain the administrative or accounting documents held by public bodies (public administrations and bodies under state control, local authorities and public establishments), which are one of its main sources information. To this end, since 2015 the Moroccan DGI has signed a number of EOI agreements with the ADII (to obtain information on the value of imports and exports, for example), the CNSS (social declaration) and OMPIC to facilitate the exchange of information between the DGI and its partners using a secure and dematerialised platform. Other such agreements are currently being negotiated with the Currency Office and the Treasury (*Office des Changes et la Trésorerie Générale du Royaume*), which already provides information under the right to information procedure on exports and the value of public contracts, and with the BAM.

295. It also exercises its right to information with natural or legal persons carrying out a taxable activity, including the liberal professions, in order to obtain accounting documentation (invoices, delivery notes, accounting entries, etc.), legal documents (such as contracts) and/or all other documents (written, registers, files, etc.) that they hold, whether in hard or electronic copy.

296. In practice, the SREF has two officers dedicated to EOI procedures within the BRR, based in Casablanca. At the request of the SREF sent by email, the two BRR officers exercise the right to information on the public administrations and on third parties, in Casablanca and elsewhere in Morocco. When the information holder is in the Rabat-Casablanca area, these officers hand-deliver the right to information notice to the concerned third party. Where the information holder is elsewhere in the Kingdom, the right to information is exercised by mail. In general, these two officers exercise the right to communication within 7 days following the request of the SREF. The information holder usually provides the requested information by mail or by hand to the BRR officers within 30 days. The information requested is then given in person to the officers of the BRR in the premises of the entities in question, or is sent by post to the DGI. Finally, the BRR provides the SREF with this information within 7 days.

297. However, over the review period, the right to information, which constitutes the main power for the tax administration to obtain information from third parties, did not include a compulsory time limit to reply. Therefore, not all the requests were answered during this period (see above). The introduction of a compulsory time limit from 1 January 2016 should reinforce the efficiency of the right to information. It is recommended that Morocco ensure the monitoring of the practical implementation of the new provision relating to the right to information, including the compulsory 30-day time limit to reply.

298. The Moroccan authorities have indicated that in a scenario where the third party holding information declined to respond to a right to information notice, or where only the taxpayer under investigation held this information, the tax administration could, where necessary, obtain the information directly from the taxpayer or the third party by exercising its right of inspection. It would be exercised by an officer of the DRI at the request of the SREF. However, Morocco has not used this power in practice to answer an EOI request.

299. Lastly, the Moroccan authority have also specified that they could carry out an onsite tax audit, if, despite the sanctions applied, the holder of the information declined to provide it. In fact, these taxpayers are listed by the BRR and presented to the compliance checking department (*Service de la Programmation des Vérifications*) as being taxpayers presenting a tax risk.

300. The table below shows the effective use of the right to information, right of inspection and accounting inspections in Morocco during the review period, for both domestic use and for EOI purposes.

	2012	2013	2014
Number of rights to information carried out	753	15 149	11 987
Number of rights of inspection carried out	3	16	7
Number of onsite audits carried out	1 774	1 415	1 439

Use of information-gathering measures in the absence of domestic tax interest (ToR B.1.3)

301. The concept of "domestic tax interest" describes situations in which a contracting party can only provide information to another contracting party if it has an interest in gathering such information for its own needs.

302. Article 214 of the Moroccan Tax Code institutes a right to information in order to "assess and audit the taxes and duties payable by third parties". This applies to all the taxes and duties contained in the Moroccan Tax Code, including income and sales taxes. Although information requested by Morocco's partners is not intended for the assessment of tax in Morocco, the tax authorities are still empowered to use the right to information solely for information exchange purposes.

303. The use of domestic information-gathering powers for exchange of information purposes, by the application of Article 214 of the Moroccan Tax Code, is based on information exchange agreements and their enforcement in Moroccan domestic law. The preamble to the Moroccan Constitution states that:

> "[…] the Kingdom of Morocco, a united State, totally sovereign, belonging to the Grand Maghreb, reaffirms that which follows and commits itself […] – to accord the international conventions it has duly ratified, within the framework of the provisions of the Constitution and the laws of the Kingdom, respecting its immutable national identity, on publication of such conventions, precedence over the country's domestic law and consequently to harmonise the relevant provisions of national law".

304. Thus, international conventions concluded and ratified by Morocco become part of Moroccan law as of publication and take precedence over Moroccan domestic law. The tax authorities are therefore required to use the right to information set forth at Article 214 of the Moroccan Tax Code in order to respond to any information request from a jurisdiction with which

Morocco has concluded and ratified a convention containing an article relating to the exchange of information. There is no provision in Moroccan law to prevent the tax authorities from using their domestic information gathering powers for information exchange purposes.

305. According to the Moroccan authorities, the provisions under which information may be gathered in order to assess or audit Moroccan taxes and duties are interpreted as being valid even where the information is intended solely for a foreign tax authority, provided that it is justified by an international convention concluded between the country concerned and Morocco.

306. In practice, the Moroccan authorities use their domestic information-gathering powers to respond to exchange of information requests when the information received is not directly available in its own files, applications or databases. In this scenario, the tax authorities generally use their right to information which enables them to obtain information from the public administrations, all persons and entities, including companies governed by the law on offshore financial centres. However, in the absence of dissuasive sanctions and binding time limit to reply, not all the requests were answered by the information holders during the review period (see above). The table below illustrates the use of right to information powers in Morocco for EOI purposes.

	Right to information powers used for EOI purposes	
	Number of notices served	Number of responses received
2012	27	23
2013	18	11
2014	20	15

307. The use of the right to information is generally enough to obtain the information required. Nevertheless, Morocco has also indicated that the tax administration could also use if needed its right of inspection or carry out a tax audit to obtain the information requested by its partners for EOI purposes.

308. In conclusion, the Moroccan authorities use the same information-gathering powers for domestic purposes and for EOI purposes. None of the comments received from Morocco's partners regarding EOI suggest that the use of their information-gathering powers by the Moroccan authorities is restricted by domestic interests.

Enforcement powers *(ToR B.1.4)*

309. Over the review period, failure to provide information and documents requested under the right to information set forth at Article 214 of the Moroccan Tax Code or the right of inspection set forth at Article 210 was punishable by a fine of MAD 2 000 (EUR 181) and, where relevant, a daily fine of MAD 100 (EUR 9) for each day's delay up to a limit of MAD 1 000 (EUR 90) (Articles 185 and 191 of the Moroccan Tax Code). During the on-site visit, Morocco has confirmed that these sanctions were not dissuasive. This is why not all the requests were answered.

310. Dahir no. 1-15-150 of the 7 rabii I 1437 (19 December 2015) enacting finances law no. 70-15 for the 2016 financial year strengthens the sanctions applicable for failure to respond within the designated timeframe to the right to information notice. Henceforth, Article 185 sanctions failure to provide the requested information within a period of 30 days following receipt of the right to information notice with a daily fine of MAD 500 (EUR 45) up to a limit of MAD 50 000 (EUR 4 500). It is recommended that Morocco ensures that the sanctions applicable for failure to respond within the designated timeframe to the right to information notice are effectively applied.

311. These penalties do not apply to government agencies or local authorities (Article 185 of the Moroccan Tax Code).

Secrecy provisions *(ToR B.1.5)*

Banking secrecy

312. All persons who, in whatever capacity, participate in the administration, direction or management of a credit institution or are employed by one, and more generally all persons who, in whatever capacity, have cause to know or use information relating to such institutions are strictly bound by professional secrecy for all matters which come to their attention, in whatever manner, under the terms of Article 44 of the Penal Code (Article 79 of Act 34-03 on credit institutions and similar organisations), and subject to the penalties set forth therein. This secrecy requirement may be lifted in those cases provided by law (Article 80).

313. Under Article 181 of the law on credit institutions and similar organisations, professional secrecy may not be invoked against Bank Al-Maghrib, the judicial authorities acting in criminal proceedings or any other authority which has concluded a bilateral tax information exchange agreement with the Kingdom of Morocco (including DTCs).

314. Pursuant to the law on offshore financial centres, any person who, in the course of their duties, participates in the administration, management or

control of an offshore bank or is employed by one is bound by professional secrecy. The secrecy requirement may be lifted in certain cases:

- if the customer or his or her assigns give their permission;
- if the customer is declared bankrupt;
- on an order from a judicial authority;
- pursuant to obligations arising from Morocco's accession to international conventions, especially relating to crime prevention (Article 26 of the law on offshore financial centres).

315. In addition, Article 214 of the Moroccan Tax Code was modified by Dahir no. 1-15-150 of the 7 rabii I 1437 (19 December 2015) enacting finances law no. 70-15 for the 2016 financial year in order to remove all ambiguity over the scope of the right to information. Henceforth, this Article sets out that "notwithstanding anything to the contrary", the tax administration can exercise its right to information powers on any person.

316. Any person bound by a professional secrecy obligation who divulges a professional secret, except where required or authorised to do so by law, is liable to imprisonment for one to six months and a fine of MAD 1 200 (EUR 108) to MAD 20 000 (EUR 1 800) by virtue of Article 446 of the Penal Code.

317. Most tax conventions signed by Morocco, except for the Multilateral Convention and the conventions negotiated after the updating of Article 26 of the OCED and UN model tax conventions, do not contain the equivalent of Article 26 (5) of the OECD Model Tax Convention. However, under Moroccan domestic law (Article 181 of the law on credit institutions and similar organisations) banking secrecy may not be invoked in connection with information exchange pursuant to a bilateral convention concluded with Morocco, nor in relation to the right to information of the tax administration (Article 214 of the Moroccan Tax Code). Furthermore, the Moroccan authorities have confirmed that they exchange banking information even where there is no reciprocal arrangement. Thus, in the absence of a measure equivalent to Article 26 (5) of the OECD Model Tax Convention, the Moroccan authorities may exchange banking information even if the requesting jurisdiction is unable to reciprocate because the tax convention between the two jurisdictions does not contain any such provision.

In practice

318. Banking secrecy cannot be invoked against the tax administration when it uses its right to information powers to obtain banking information (account number, account balance and statements) from credit establishments, whether for domestic purposes or for EOI purposes.

319. Until the end of 2015, the standard format of a right to information notice was used to gather banking information. The SREF used the two officers of the BRR in charge of information exchange, who prepared the right to information notice according to the format laid out in Article 214 of the Moroccan Tax Code and, in principle, visited one of the branches of the credit establishment in order to deliver the notice in person. When the person in question was a client of the branch being investigated, this branch would be in possession of the information needed. However, the branch had to contact its head office when the person was not a client of that particular branch. The head office then provided the required information to the requested branch. The information required was then given in person to one of the officers of the BRR on the bank's premises, or was sent by post to the BRR. Eventually, the BRR officers passed on this information to the SREF.

320. Since the 1 January 2016, a new procedure has been experimented. Periodically, the SREF transmits a list of people about whom it requires banking information, under the right to information procedures. This list is sent via a secure email connection to the dedicated email address opened by each of the credit establishments in Morocco. They are then required to provide the SREF with the information required about their clients on the list via email.

321. Over the review period, Morocco received 65 EOI requests for banking information, the details of which are shown in the table below. When the information required was provided by Morocco, its EOI partners said that the responses were generally complete. However, in 15 cases, Morocco was unable to provide the information requested. This is because it is difficult to obtain banking information when the requesting jurisdiction does not provide the bank account number or the national identity card or passport or residence permit number, or the commercial register number of the person who is the object of the EOI, given that the tax administration does not have a national database of bank account holders. Morocco also indicated that within the SREF, officers are mandated to identify the people targeted by the requesting jurisdictions using the databases to which the SREF has access. Lastly, as mentioned earlier, the BAM has built a centralised database of all bank accounts, and the tax administration has started negotiations with the BAM to obtain access to the information contained in this database. As there are only 19 banks and six offshore banks in Morocco, this should facilitate access to banking information. In addition, the change of procedure for gathering banking information has not affected the capacity of the tax authorities to identify the taxpayer from his or her first and last name and date of birth.

Year	Requests referring to			Total
	Account numbers (1)	Bank statements (2)	Accounts and statements (3)	(1)+(2)+(3)
2012	9	10	8	27
2013	4	8	6	18
2014	6	10	4	20
Total	19	28	18	65

Professional secrecy for the legal and accountancy professions

322. Attorney-client privilege is protected by Article 36 of the Dahir enacting Act 1-93-62 of 10 September 1993 organising exercise of the legal profession. It states that an attorney may not disclose any information in breach of professional secrecy. In particular, they must respect the confidentiality of criminal investigations and refrain from disclosing any information taken from files or making public any items, documents or letters relating to an on-going investigation.

323. The purpose of attorney-client privilege as defined in Moroccan law is to protect information received by an attorney for the purposes of obtaining a legal opinion in the context of an investigation. However, information not related to an investigation, including information obtained in an advisory capacity, must be disclosed to the tax authorities on request.

324. Professional secrecy for notaries is protected by Articles 24 and 25 of Act 32-09 organising the notarial profession. They state that:

> "Article 24. Notaries are bound by a professional secrecy obligation except where otherwise provided by law. The same obligation applies to their interns and employees.
>
> Article 25. Notaries are prohibited from issuing documents or excerpts from documents to persons other than those who are entitled to them by law".

325. Statutory auditors are also subject to a duty of professional secrecy, which states that: "statutory auditors as well as their collaborators are bound by professional secrecy for actions, instruments and information brought to their knowledge in the performance of their duties" (Article 177 of the law on limited companies).

326. Any breach of professional secrecy by an attorney, notary or a statutory auditor is punishable pursuant to Article 446 of the Penal Code.

327. As mentioned above, Article 214 of the Moroccan Tax Code has been clarified by the 2016 finances law so that "notwithstanding anything

to the contrary", professional secrecy cannot be invoked to oppose the right to information of the tax administration. However, the same article sets out that, "with regards to liberal professions whose work involves the provision of legal, tax or accounting services, the right to information cannot mean that the entire file will be communicated". In other words, these professions are duty bound to respond to the right to information notices of the tax administration providing the notice states which documents are required, including if more than one document is required. This interpretation has been confirmed by the representatives of these professions met during the onsite visit. They also explained that in practice, even before the clarification provided to Article 214 of the Moroccan Tax Code, they did not invoke their professional secrecy obligation in the case of right to information notices from the tax authorities.

Conclusion

328. Lawyers, notaries and statutory auditors are bound by a professional secrecy obligation. Since 1 January 2016, the right to information of the tax administration is expressly exercised with regards to all persons, "notwithstanding anything to the contrary". Attorneys, notaries and statutory auditors cannot invoke their professional secrecy obligation to refuse to respond to a request of information of the tax administration. During the onsite visit, these professionals explained that in practice they already interpreted the former version of Article 214 in this way. They also indicated that the only limit to the right to information is the client-attorney privilege as part of legal proceedings and the fact that, as stated in Article 214, the tax administration does not have the right to request the client's entire file. However, they have confirmed that the fact to request many documents that are listed in the notice is not interpreted as requiring the entire client's file, including if, when taken as a whole, providing all the documents requested would de facto result in providing the client's entire file. There were no comments from peers that suggested that the professional secrecy obligation of attorneys, notaries or statutory auditors had ever been invoked to the tax authorities beyond the limits allowed for by the standard.

Conclusion and factors underlying the recommendations

Phase 1 determination
The element is in place.

Phase 2 rating	
Largely Compliant	
Factors underlying the recommendations	**Recommendations**
During the review period, the right to information of the tax administration, which is its main power to obtain information from third parties, did not include a compulsory time limit to reply. Moreover, the sanctions applicable for failure to respond to the right to information were not dissuasive. However, the provision relating to the right to information has been modified recently. Since 1 January 2016, the right to information includes a compulsory 30-day time limit to reply and dissuasive sanctions.	Morocco should monitor the effective application of the new provisions regarding the right to information in practice.

B.2. Notification requirements and rights and safeguards

The rights and safeguards (e.g. notification, appeal rights) that apply to persons in the requested jurisdiction should be compatible with effective exchange of information.

329. Rights and safeguards should not unduly prevent or delay the effective exchange of information. For example, notification procedures should allow exceptions to prior notification (e.g. in cases where the information request is very urgent or where notification is liable to comprises the chances of success of the investigation carried out by the requesting jurisdiction).

Rights and safeguards should not unduly prevent or delay exchange of information (ToR B.2.1)

330. There is no provision in Moroccan domestic law which requires a person to be informed when they are the subject of an information request, including in the framework of international administrative assistance.

331. In practice, there have been no restrictions to access to information relating to the notification procedure of a taxpayer. None of the comments on the EOI process received from Morocco's partners suggested that the provision of the required information is hindered or slowed in Morocco as a result of the rights or protections accorded to taxpayers.

Conclusion and factors underlying the recommendations

Phase 1 determination
The element is in place.

Phase 2 rating
Compliant.

C. Exchange of information

Overview

332. Jurisdictions generally cannot exchange information for tax purposes unless they have a legal basis or mechanisms for doing so. In Morocco, the legal authority to exchange information is derived from multilateral and bilateral mechanisms (double tax conventions). This section of the report assesses whether Morocco has a network of exchange of information (EOI) agreements which entitle it to achieve effective exchange of information.

333. Morocco has an extensive network of EOI agreements in the form of bilateral or multilateral conventions. Morocco is a signatory to the multilateral Convention on Mutual Administrative Assistance in Tax Matters (Multilateral Convention, which is not yet ratified) and to the Convention between the states of the Arab Maghreb Union for the avoidance of double taxation and mutual assistance with respect to taxes on income (Arab Maghreb Union tax convention).

334. Morocco currently has a network of information exchange agreements covering 122 jurisdictions, of which 56 are in force. Considering all the information exchange agreements concluded by Morocco, the country has information exchange agreements compliant with the standard with 120 jurisdictions (the agreements with Bahrain and Malaysia are not in line with the standard) and can already exchange information in compliance with the standard with 46 of them. However, more than two years after their signature, eight tax agreements and the Multilateral Convention are not ratified by Morocco yet. Therefore, Morocco is recommended to ensure that these tax agreements signed before 2014 as well as the Multilateral Convention signed on 21 May 2013 enter into force rapidly.

335. Morocco's network of agreements covers all its major economic partners, EU and OECD Member States and a large number of financial centres and Global Forum members. Morocco has never declined to conclude an information exchange agreement with another jurisdiction.

336. All mechanisms for exchanging information include provisions concerned with confidentiality, and Moroccan domestic legislation also contains provisions on this subject. They apply equally to the information and documents concerned by the request received by the Moroccan competent authority and to the responses provided to the treaty partner.

337. Likewise, all the agreements concluded by Morocco contain provisions which protect the rights and safeguards of taxpayers and third parties.

338. Over the review period, Morocco received 182 EOI requests from 12 treaty partners. Despite this high number, the EOI requests were dealt with in an ad hoc manner, involving a number of departments that were not dedicated specifically to this task. Thus, as a result of the complex organisation, inadequate steering, non-documented processes and non-dedicated resources, Morocco was unable to process these EOI requests from its partners efficiently and in a timely manner. In addition, Morocco's treaty partners were not provided with a status update on their requests where a response was not forthcoming within 90 days of the request being made, and sometimes even after the partner had repeated their request. The peers indicated that 58 EOI requests did not receive a response during the review period and that around 15 files had been closed as a result of responses arriving too late to be useful. Although the recent creation of a EOI department and the writing of an EOI manual should improve the way EOI requests are processed, two recommendations have been made for Morocco. Firstly, Morocco is recommended to ensure that all EOI requests from its partners receive a timely response, and that a status update on their requests is systematically provided when it is not possible to provide a response within 90 days of the request being received. Secondly, Morocco is recommended to put in place a suitable organisation and monitoring system for the processing of EOI requests, in particularly by adopting internal deadlines for processing requests and a documented process, in order to ensure that in all cases, partners receive timely responses to their requests.

C.1. Exchange of information mechanisms

Exchange of information mechanisms should allow for effective exchange of information.

339. Morocco has an extensive network of information exchange agreements in the form of bilateral or multilateral conventions. Morocco has been a signatory to the Multilateral Convention since 21 May 2013, meaning that it has an agreement compliant with the standard with 54 jurisdictions with which it did not previously have an information exchange agreement.

340. Morocco is also a party to the Arab Maghreb Union tax convention, the other parties to which are Algeria, Libya, Mauritania and Tunisia.

341. Morocco therefore has an information exchange agreement with 122 jurisdictions, of which 56 are in force. Considering all the information exchange agreements concluded by Morocco, the country has information exchange agreements compliant with the standard with 120 jurisdictions[11] and can already exchange information in compliance with the standard with 46[12] of them.

342. Morocco has also initialled a further 1 double tax conventions (DTC) with Azerbaijan, Bangladesh, Bosnia-Herzegovina, Central African Republic, Chad, Ethiopia, Gambia, Georgia, Mexico, Republic of Congo, Seychelles, South Africa, Sudan, Thailand and Turkmenistan.

343. Morocco is currently negotiating information exchange agreements with Cyprus[13], Democratic Republic of Congo, Equatorial Guinea, Ghana, Rwanda and Sweden.

Standard of foreseeable relevance (ToR C.1.1)

344. The international standard in information exchange assumes that information should be exchanged upon request to the widest possible extent. However, it does not allow "fishing expeditions", meaning speculative requests for information which appear to have no clear link with an on-going audit or investigation. The balance between these two competing aspects is expressed in the concept of "foreseeable relevance" contained in Article 26 (1) of the OECD Model Tax Convention, which states:

---

11. The agreements with Bahrain and Malaysia do not comply with the standard.
12. Algeria, Austria, Belgium, Bulgaria, Canada, China (People's Republic of), Côte d'Ivoire, Croatia, Czech Republic, Denmark, Egypt, Finland, Former Yugoslav Republic of Macedonia (FYROM), Gabon, Greece, Guinea, Hungary, India, Indonesia, Ireland, Italy, Jordan, Kuwait, Latvia, Lebanon, Libya, Luxembourg, Mali, Malta, Mauritania, Oman, Pakistan, Poland, Portugal, Qatar, Federation of Russia (Russia), Senegal, Singapore, South Korea, Syrian Arab Republic (Syria), Tunisia, Turkey, Ukraine, United Arab Emirates, United States, Viet Nam.
13. Note by Turkey: The information contained in this document with reference to "Cyprus" relates to the southern part of the Island. There is no single authority representing both Turkish and Greek Cypriot people on the Island. Turkey recognises the Turkish Republic of Northern Cyprus (TRNC). Until a lasting and equitable solution is found within the context of the United Nations, Turkey shall preserve its position concerning the "Cyprus issue".

    Note by all the European Union Member States of the OECD and by the European Union: The Republic of Cyprus is recognised by all members of the United Nations with the exception of Turkey. The information in this document relates to the area under the effective control of the Government of the Republic of Cyprus.

> "The competent authorities of the Contracting States shall exchange such information as is foreseeably relevant for carrying out the provisions of this Convention or to the administration or enforcement of the domestic laws concerning taxes of every kind and description imposed on behalf of the Contracting States, or of their political subdivisions or local authorities, insofar as the taxation thereunder is not contrary to the Convention. The exchange of information is not restricted by Articles 1 and 2."

345. Only a handful of treaties concluded by Morocco contain the words "foreseeably relevant"[14]. Most of the treaties signed by Morocco contain the term "necessary". The term "necessary" is considered in the commentary on Article 26 of the OECD Model Convention as being equivalent in effect to "foreseeably relevant" with regard to the exchange of information. Morocco confirms that it supports this interpretation and that it treats the expression "useful information" which occurs in the treaty with France in the same way. These treaties may therefore be considered to comply with the standard of foreseeable relevance.

346. A certain number of treaties (those with Bahrain, France, Germany, Malaysia, Netherlands, Norway, Romania, Spain and United Kingdom) restrict the exchange of information to application of the "provisions of this convention". As they do not therefore permit the exchange of information not referred to in the convention, they do not comply with the international standard.

347. However, France, Germany, Netherlands, Norway, Romania, Spain and United Kingdom are covered by the Multilateral Convention. Thus, only Bahrain and Malaysia do not have an agreement with Morocco which complies with the standard.

348. The tax convention with Switzerland concluded on 31 March 1993 does not contain an exchange of information clause. Switzerland is a signatory to the Multilateral Convention.

349. In practice, Morocco indicated that applies the principle of foreseeable relevance without restriction. None of the comments from peers suggested that during the review period, Morocco declined to respond to an EOI request on the grounds that the request was not foreseeably relevant.

In respect of all persons *(ToR C.1.2)*

350. Effective information exchange presupposes that the obligation of a jurisdiction to provide information should not be limited by the residence or

14. Those with Estonia, Former Yugoslav Republic of Macedonia (FYROM), Guinea, Ireland, Lithuania and Mali and the Multilateral Convention.

nationality of either the person to whom the requested information relates, or the person who possesses or holds the information requested. For this reason, the international standard in information exchange states that the mechanisms for exchange can permit an exchange of information concerning all persons.

351. Article 26 (1) of the OECD Model Tax Convention states that "the exchange of information is not restricted by Articles 1 and 2". Article 1 defines the personal scope of the Convention. The agreements concluded with 106 jurisdictions are compliant in all respects with the OECD Model Tax Convention, through either a bilateral agreement or the Multilateral Convention. However, 19 bilateral agreements concluded by Morocco do not contain the phrase from the model (those with Belgium, Burkina Faso, Canada, Côte d'Ivoire, Denmark, Egypt, Italy, Iran, Jordan, Luxembourg, Pakistan, Poland, Serbia, Singapore, Ukraine, United States, Vietnam and Yemen, and the Arab Maghreb Union tax convention). The article on information exchange in these agreements nevertheless applies to both residents and non-residents of the parties, since it applies to "the provisions of this Convention, or those of the domestic laws of the Contracting States relating to the taxes covered by the Convention, insofar as the taxation thereunder is not contrary to the Convention".

352. These treaties do not therefore restrict information exchange to residents only, since domestic tax law applies to all taxpayers (and third parties where access to information is concerned), whether resident or not (for example, non-residents are liable to tax on their income of domestic origin). An exchange of information concerning all persons is therefore possible under the terms of these treaties. The Moroccan authorities confirm that they support this interpretation.

353. Finally, 8 bilateral agreements[15] concluded by Morocco do not contain the phrase from the OECD Model Tax Convention; the wording of the article in these agreements relating to information exchange states that the agreement applies only to "the taxes covered by the Convention" and not to the Contracting States' domestic law. In these cases the agreements do not apply to all persons (and non-residents in particular) and do not therefore comply with the standard. However, these jurisdictions (with the exception of Bahrain and Malaysia) are covered by the Multilateral Convention, which is compliant with the standard.

354. In practice, the peers experienced no restriction to exchange of information based on the grounds that the person in question was not resident in Morocco.

15. With Bahrain, France, Germany, Malaysia, Netherlands, Norway, Spain and United Kingdom.

Obligation to exchange all types of information (ToR C.1.3)

355. Jurisdictions cannot undertake effective information exchange if they are unable to exchange information which is held by financial institutions, nominees or persons acting in an agency or fiduciary capacity or because the information relates to ownership interests in a person.

356. Article 26 (5) of the OECD Model Convention provides that a contracting state may not decline to supply information solely because it is held by a bank, other financial institution, nominee or person acting in an agency or a fiduciary capacity, or because it relates to ownership interests in a person.

357. Morocco has concluded 14 agreements (with Albania, Cameroon, Estonia, Former Yugoslav Republic of Macedonia (FYROM), Guinea, Guinea Bissau, India (amending protocol), Ireland, Lithuania, Mali, Mauritius, Sao Tomé-et-Principe and Saudi Arabia as well as the Multilateral Convention) which contain provisions equivalent to Article 26 (4) and (5) of the OECD Model Tax Convention.

358. However, Moroccan domestic law does not contain any restriction on the exchange of information with its partners: the competent authority can provide them with all types of information, even if the information exchange agreement does not contain the equivalent of Article 26 (4) and (5) of the OECD Model Tax Convention. Morocco has confirmed that it does not apply the principle of reciprocity; thus, in the absence of the equivalent of Article 26 (4) and (5) of the OECD Model Tax Convention, the Moroccan authorities can exchange banking information even if the requesting jurisdiction cannot exchange such information because paragraphs 4 and 5 do not appear in the tax convention between the two jurisdictions.

359. In practice, Morocco has never declined to assist an EOI partner on the grounds that the information required is held by financial institutions, nominees or persons acting in an agency or a fiduciary capacity, or because the information relates to ownership interests in a person, as has been confirmed in the comments received by the peers.

Absence of domestic tax interest (ToR C.1.4)

360. The concept of domestic tax interest describes situations in which a contracting party can only provide information to another contracting party if it has an interest in obtaining the desired information for its own tax purposes. Inability to provide information which is based on any such domestic tax interest does not comply with the international standard. The contracting parties should use domestic information-gathering powers, even if they are used solely for the purpose of obtaining and providing information for the other contracting party.

361. Most of the agreements concluded by Morocco do not contain the equivalent of Article 26 (4) of the OECD Model Tax Convention, which requires contracting states to use their information-gathering measures to obtain the requested information even though they may not need it for their own tax purposes. However, Morocco is in a position, even without this paragraph, to exchange information with its partners without reference to a domestic tax interest.

362. In practice, Morocco has never declined to assist an EOI partner on the grounds of an absence of domestic interest, as has been confirmed in the comments received by the peers.

Absence of dual criminality principles (ToR C.1.5)

363. The dual criminality principle states that assistance can only be provided if the matter under investigation (and prompting the request for information) would constitute a criminal matter in the requested country if it had arisen in that country. If it is to be meaningful, information exchange must not be restricted by the enforcement of a dual criminality principle.

364. None of the information exchange mechanisms established by Morocco provide for the application of the dual criminality principle in order to restrict the exchange of information. The peers found no instances where Morocco has declined an EOI request on the grounds of the dual criminality principle.

Exchange of information in both civil and criminal tax matters (ToR C.1.6)

365. Communicating information may be necessary for both tax and criminal purposes. The international standard is not limited to exchanges of information for criminal purposes and may also include exchanges for tax purposes.

366. All information exchange mechanisms concluded by Morocco provide for the exchange of information for both criminal and civil matters. The comments of the peers do not suggest that Morocco would decline to provide assistance in the case of a criminal or a civil tax matter.

Provide information in the specific form requested (ToR C.1.7)

367. In certain cases, a contracting party may need to receive information in a specific form in order to meet its evidentiary standards or other legal requirements. These forms may include witness statements and certified copies of original documents. The requested party may decline to provide

information in the specific form requested if, for example, it is unknown or not authorised in its administrative practice. Declining to provide information in the requested form does not affect the requirement to provide the information.

368. There are no restrictions in the information exchange mechanisms established by Morocco that would prevent the Moroccan authorities from providing the information in the requested form as long as it complies with their administrative practice. The peers indicated that the form of the responses they received was adequate.

In force (ToR C.1.8)

369. The exchange of information cannot occur unless a jurisdiction has information exchange mechanisms in force. Where such mechanisms have been signed, the international standard requires a jurisdiction to complete the measures needed for them to take effect.

370. In Morocco, all treaties of a tax nature, whether double tax conventions, information exchange agreements, protocols amending existing conventions or multilateral agreements, must be ratified by Parliament.

371. Morocco has concluded information exchange agreements with 122 jurisdictions; 46 of them are compliant with the standard and in force. The agreement with Yemen was ratified by Morocco on 18 February 2009, but is not still in force as Yemen has not yet finalised its ratification process. Morocco indicated during the phase 1 review that the agreements with Burkina Faso, Cameroon, Côte d'Ivoire, Estonia, Guinea, Lithuania, Mali and Qatar (DTC revised) will be ratified soon. The agreements with Cote d'Ivoire, Guinea and Mali entered into force on 7 March 2016, 15 January 2016 and 3 June 2016 respectively. However, eight tax agreements signed before 2014 have still not been ratified by Morocco, as shown in the table below:

Jurisdiction	Date the tax agreement was signed
Burkina Faso	18/05/2012
Cameroon	07/09/2012
Estonia	25/09/2013
India (amending protocol)	08/08/2013
Iran	25/02/2008
Lithuania	19/04/2013
Qatar (revision)	27/12/2013
Serbia	06/06/2013

Cameroon, Estonia, India, Lithuania and Serbia have finalised the ratification procedure of their agreements with Morocco. Burkina Faso, Iran and Qatar have not ratified their agreements with Morocco yet.

372. In addition, the Multilateral Convention, which was signed by Morocco on 21 May 2013, is still not in force in Morocco. This Convention allows Morocco to have an agreement compliant with the standard with 54 jurisdictions with which it does not have an EOI agreement. The ratification procedure is still ongoing. The Moroccan Parliament approved the ratification of the Multilateral Convention on 19 January 2016. The Dahir no. 1-16-06 promulgating the law no. 30-14 approving the Multilateral Convention as adopted by the two houses of Parliament was published on 18 February 2016 in the official Bulletin. In order to finalise the ratification procedure, the project of "ratification instruments" must be submitted to the royal seal and the ratification instrument must be deposited with the Coordinating Body of the Multilateral Convention.

373. More than two years after their signature, eight tax agreements and the Multilateral Convention are not ratified by Morocco yet. Therefore, Morocco is recommended to ensure that these tax agreements signed before 2014 as well as the Multilateral Convention signed on 21 May 2013 enter into force rapidly.

374. In practice, the ratification procedure in Morocco starts once the agreement has been signed by the Minister of Foreign Affairs or the authority awarded full powers of signature. The signed agreement is passed from the Legal Affairs and Treaties Directorate (*Direction des Affaires Juridiques et des Traités,* DAJT) to the Ministry for Foreign Affairs and Co-operation within the General Secretariat of the Government (SGG), accompanied by an explanatory note presenting the agreement and the draft "letter of ratification". The SGG sets out the timetable for ratification and includes the draft ratification law on the agenda of the Government cabinet meeting. Once it has been examined by the cabinet, the draft ratification law is put to Parliament for approval (House of Representatives and then House of Counsellors). After the adoption of the ratification by Parliament and its publication in the Official Bulletin, the project of "ratification instruments" is submitted to the royal seal. The ratification instruments are then exchanged in the case of bilateral agreements, or placed with a depositary for multilateral agreements and then the agreement is published in the Official Bulletin. The Moroccan authorities said that this procedure usually takes two years.

In effect (ToR C.1.9)

375. In order for information exchange to be effective, the contracting parties must take the necessary measures to comply with their commitments.

Once a treaty or agreement has come into force, Morocco does not need to take any additional measure in order for it to be effective.

Conclusion and factors underlying the recommendations

Phase 1 determination	
The element is in place, but certain aspects of its legal implementation needs improvement	
Factors underlying the recommendations	**Recommendations**
8 of the tax agreements signed by Morocco before 2014 as well as the Multilateral Convention signed on 21 May 2013, which offers Morocco 54 potential new EOI partners, are still not in force in Morocco.	Morocco must ensure that the EOI agreements it signs enter into force rapidly.

Phase 2 rating
Largely compliant.

C.2. Mechanisms for exchanging information with all relevant partners

> The jurisdictions' network of information exchange mechanisms should cover all relevant partners.

376. According to the international standard, jurisdictions should be able to exchange information with all relevant partners, meaning partners interested in concluding an EOI agreement. Agreements cannot be concluded solely with partners of no economic importance. If a jurisdiction refuses to conclude or negotiate agreements with partners, especially those which have reasonable grounds for seeking information from that jurisdiction in order to properly administer and enforce their tax laws, that fact may indicate a lack of commitment to implementing the standards.

377. Morocco has an extensive network of EOI agreements, including 66 bilateral agreements and two multilateral agreements, namely the Multilateral Convention (which guarantees Morocco standard-compliant exchanges of information with 54 new jurisdictions with which it has no other EOI agreement) and the Arab Maghreb Union tax convention, the other signatories to which are Algeria, Libya, Mauritania and Tunisia. Morocco's network of EOI agreements therefore currently covers 122 jurisdictions, of which 120 comply with the standard. Morocco therefore has a network compliant with the standard covering all its relevant partners.

378. Morocco has stated that its main economic partners are France and Spain. In 2013, 40% of Morocco's exportations and 26% of Morocco's importations were carried out with these two partners.

379. Morocco's network of EOI agreements covers:

- All the OECD Member States;
- All the EU Member States;
- All the members of the G20;
- 107 Global Forum jurisdictions.

380. Morocco's policy is to give priority to its economic partners with which it has not yet concluded an international tax convention, especially other African countries. Since 2009, Morocco has used a model tax convention with an article 26 on exchange of information equivalent in all respects to the OECD Model Tax Convention, including the equivalent of Article 26 (4) and (5) of the Model Convention.

381. Morocco has indicated that it has started the ratification procedure for DTCs with Albania, Burkina Faso, Cameroon, Estonia, Guinea-Bissau, Lithuania, Mauritius, Qatar (Revised), Sao Tome and Principe, Saudi Arabia, Serbia, Slovenia, and Yemen.

382. Morocco has also initialled a further 15 double tax conventions with Azerbaijan, Bangladesh, Bosnia-Herzegovina, Chad, Central African Republic, Ethiopia, Gambia, Georgia, Mexico, Republic of Congo, Seychelles, South Africa, Sudan, Thailand and Turkmenistan.

383. Morocco is currently negotiating information exchange agreements containing an information exchange clause in compliance with the standard with Cyprus, Democratic Republic of Congo, Equatorial Guinea, Ghana, Rwanda and Sweden.

Conclusion and factors underlying the recommendations

Phase 1 determination	
The element is in place.	
Factors underlying the recommendations	**Recommendations**
	Morocco should continue to extend its EOI network in compliance with the standard.

Phase 2 rating
Compliant.

C.3. Confidentiality

> The jurisdictions' mechanisms for exchange of information should have adequate provisions to ensure the confidentiality of information received.

Information received: disclosure, use and safeguards (ToR C.3.1)

384. Governments could not become involved in exchanging information without being certain that the details communicated will be used solely for the purposes specified in the relevant information exchange agreement and that they will be kept confidential. Information exchange mechanisms should thus contain provisions indicating exactly the persons to whom the information may be circulated. Furthermore, the domestic legislation in force in the countries concerned usually contains strict regulations on protecting the confidentiality of information gathered for tax purposes.

385. Each of the EOI agreements concluded by Morocco contains a confidentiality clause compliant with Article 26 (2) of the OECD Model Tax Convention, which states that:

> "Any information received under paragraph 1 by a Contracting State shall be treated as secret in the same manner as information obtained under the domestic laws of that State and shall be disclosed only to persons or authorities (including courts and administrative bodies) concerned with the assessment or collection of, the enforcement or prosecution in respect of, the determination of appeals in relation to the taxes referred to in paragraph 1, or the oversight of the above. Such persons or authorities shall use the information only for such purposes. They may disclose the information in public court proceedings or in judicial decisions."

386. In addition, Moroccan domestic law contains rules designed to guarantee the confidentiality of exchanged information. Under Article 246 of the Moroccan Tax Code, all persons who, in the performance of their duties, are involved in the assessment, control, collection or disputation of taxes or duties is bound by professional secrecy. There are exceptions to the rule, in particular for other Moroccan administration and the judicial authorities. Exchanged information may be disclosed only on an order of the competent judge.

387. Professional secrecy is defined in Article 446 of the Moroccan Penal Code, which states that all persons who are entrusted with secrets by virtue of their status or profession or function are prohibited from disclosing them. The penalties for non-compliance are imprisonment for one month to six months and a fine of MAD1 200 to 20 000 (EUR 108 to 1 800).

388. In addition, Article 18 of Dahir 1-58-008 of 24 February 1958 on the civil service regulations states that "irrespective of the rules relating to

professional secrecy set forth in the Penal Code, all civil servants are bound by a professional secrecy obligation for everything which concerns facts or information that come to their knowledge in the performance or in connection with the performance of their duties".

Other information exchanged (ToR C.3.2)

389. The provisions concerning confidentiality which are included both in the relevant agreements and in Moroccan domestic legislation do not distinguish between information received in reply to a request or information that forms part of the request. These provisions apply in the same manner to requests, attached documents, and all communications between the jurisdictions involved in the exchange.

In Practice

390. In general, the Moroccan DGI has a global confidentiality and data protection policy that it applies within the context of its activities. Confidentiality and data protection are guaranteed at a number of levels, with even more stringent conditions when it comes to information exchange.

391. Morocco has produced a national directive on the security of information systems, based on the ISO 27000 standard. This directive governs the national policy on security of information systems which also applies to all departments of the DGI. It requires prior authorisation so that only authorised persons have access to the infrastructures and applications of the DGI. The information system has antiviral protection, an information systems continuity plan is in place and an internal audit of the DGI's information system's compliance with the above-mentioned directive is being carried out. In this context, the computers of the competent authority are protected by anti-virus software, passwords are required to access the operating system and a second password is required to access the email system. Similarly, a password is required to access the SIT system. The passwords must be complex and have to be changed every six months. If computers are unused for a period of time defined by the information systems security department, the screensaver is automatically activated and the password must be re-entered to regain access to the operating system. This policy is underpinned by the presence of the information security charter, which specifies best practices to follow and the obligations of the officers in terms of use of computers, in the desktop of the computer.

392. In addition, access to the DGI premises is secured. The building that houses the competent authorities is protected by CCTV, the recordings are kept for between one and six months depending on the how sensitive the premises are. A security officer and a receptionist are present at reception

and entrance to the building is via security gates. Each visitor must identify himself at reception, provide ID and be accompanied once he has passed through the security gates. The officers of the DGI have badges that allow them to open the security gates, and only one person at a time may go through them. The premises of the competent authorities are situated on one of the upper floors. The office door is always locked and the department head is the keyholder. Access to this office is strictly limited to the head of the SREF and the three officers working for it. Inside the office, EOI requests are placed in a locked cupboard. A clean desk policy is in place. Concerning access to the DGI data centre, which is located in the same premises, only authorised persons with an access badge and an access code can enter. The data centre is also protected by CCTV.

393. With regards to the recruitment of officers of the Moroccan tax administration, the human resources department investigates the background of future officers, in particular their administrative and criminal records. Each officer receives six months of basic training which, since 2008, includes a module on the obligations and duties of public officials as well as a module on the ethics of the DGI. The latter lays out the 12 rules governing the key duties of DGI officers. In particular, they are reminded that the information to which they have access during their work must remain strictly confidential and is reserved for strictly professional use only (rules 5 and 6). In addition, they are reminded of the rules relating to the security of computer equipment and software (rule 10), data protection and information (rule 11) and the security of online communications and email (rule 12). They are also reminded of the sanctions in place for any breach of these rules. Tax auditors and the officers of the SREF and BRR are sworn officials and must take an oath. As part of their duties, they may be required to undergo training on information exchange, on quality standards and on ethics. In addition, regular training is given on computer safety as shown in the table below:

Year	Subject	Number of participants
2012	Email	23
2013	Security of Information Systems (IS)	37
	Governance of IS	3
2014	Security of Information Systems (IS)	607
	Governance of IS	2
2015	Security of Information Systems (IS)	17
	Governance of IS	1
2016 (April)	Security of Information Systems (IS)	15
Total		705

394. The recruitment of the officers of the SREF is based on more specific characteristics because of the sensitive nature of the information to which these officers have access. SREF officers are employees who are familiar with cross-referencing and EOI procedures and who have been trained in the inherent risks of handing data transmitted by treaty partners. The department heads are responsible for the proper functioning of their department and thus for the respect of confidentiality rules. Lastly, when an officer leaves the department, the head of department has to immediately inform the information services department so that all access and authorisation of this officer is deactivated, and the officer must hand in his or her badge and any equipment belonging to the DGI.

395. EOI requests from Morocco's treaty partners can be received by post or by email. When the request is received by post, it is immediately dated and stamped Confidential. Movement of the EOI request between the Central Office and the various competent authorities is the responsibility of officers from the internal post department who hand-deliver the sealed requests and require a signature. When the request is received by email, this can only be sent to the professional email address of one of the listed competent authorities. When gathering requested information, the EOI request, its content or the fact that the information is being gathered for EOI purposes are never communicated to third parties, other administrations, or any officers of the DGI other than the competent authorities and the officers of the SREF and the SCFI.

396. Over the review period, Morocco indicated that no breaches in confidentiality rules had been reported and then sanctioned. However, Morocco has indicated that, if such breaches are identified, an investigation would be immediately carried out by the tax services inspection department. A detailed report would be written by this department and then submitted to the Director General of Taxes. The report would present the irregularities committed and propose the sanctions to be taken against the concerned officer. Depending of the severity of the breach, these sanctions vary from a warning to temporary suspension, hearing before the disciplinary council and prosecution. Such sanctions are applied in Morocco for other breaches of their obligations by officers of the DGI (duty of probity, respect for superiors, obligation to provide a service, etc.) as shown by the table below.

	2012	2013	2014	2015	2016 (April)
Number of disciplinary sanctions	20	11	9	15	4

397. While each department head must ensure that confidentiality rules are respected in his or her own department, external monitoring is performed by the Audit and Inspection Division (*Division de l'Audit et de l'Inspection*, DAI) which reports directly to the Director-General of Taxes. The DAI

indicated that, when performing its audit and general inspection, it ensures that security and confidentiality rules are respected by checking if the policies and guidance relating to data security and confidentiality are followed in the audited service. However, no topical audit on this subject has yet been carried out. In addition, the DAI indicated that a guide to internal audits was being finalised and that risks relating to confidentiality should soon be documented. The table below illustrates the number of audits and inspections carried out by the DAI over the review period.

Year	Number of audits and inspections
2012	36
2013	29
2014	48

398. The organisation and procedures in place and in operation during the onsite visit to Morocco guarantee the respect of confidentiality in the processing of EOI requests.

Conclusion and factors underlying the recommendations

Phase 1 determination
The element is in place.

Phase 2 rating
Compliant.

C.4. Rights and safeguards of taxpayers and third parties

The exchange of information mechanisms should respect the rights and safeguards of taxpayers and third parties.

Exceptions to the requirement to provide information (ToR C.4.1)

399. The international standard allows jurisdictions that have been asked to provide information not to do so in certain very specific situations. Inter alia, a request for information may be declined if the requested information could reveal confidential information protected by attorney-client privilege, which is part of the legal system of many countries.

400. However, communications between attorneys and their clients are protected by Article 36 of the Dahir enacting Act 1-93-62 of 10 September 1993 organising exercise of the legal profession, which states that an attorney must respect the confidentiality of criminal investigations and not refrain

from disclosing any information taken from files or make public any items, documents or letters relating to an on-going investigation.

401. All the double taxation conventions concluded by Morocco contain a provision equivalent to the exception provided for in Article 26 (3) of the OECD Model Tax Convention, which allows a State to refuse to exchange certain types of information, including information which would disclose any trade, business, industrial or professional secret or trade process. However, the term "professional secret" is not defined in the DTCs and therefore, considering the provision of Article 3(2) of the DTCs, this term would derive its meaning from the domestic laws of Morocco. As noted in part B.1.5 of this report, notaries and statutory auditors are covered by professional secrecy, which was not fully consistent with the standard However, the modification made to Article 214 of the Moroccan Tax Code clarified that the professional secrecy obligations of attorneys, notaries and statutory auditors could not be invoked against the administration in a right to information procedure, and this "notwithstanding anything to the contrary" in the Moroccan laws. Lastly, in practice, none of the comments received by peers suggests that Morocco is unable to gather information from these professions for EOI purposes.

Conclusion and factors underlying the recommendations

Phase 1 determination
The element is in place.

Phase 2 rating
Compliant.

C.5. Timeliness of responses to requests for information

> The jurisdiction should provide information under its network of agreements in a timely manner.

Response within 90 days (ToR C.5.1)

402. In order for exchange of information to be effective it needs to be provided in a timeframe that allows tax authorities to apply the information to the relevant cases. If a response is provided but only after a significant lapse of time, the information may no longer be of use to the requesting authorities. This is particularly important in the context of international co-operation as cases in this area must be of sufficient importance to warrant making a request.

403. There are no measures in Moroccan legislation or in its EOI framework regarding responses or timeframes within which responses must be provided. As such, there is no restriction on the capacity of the Moroccan competent authorities to respond to EOI requests within 90 days of receipt of the request, either by providing the requested information or by providing a status update on the request.

404. Over the review period (from 1 January 2012 to 31 December 2014), Morocco received 182 EOI requests (72 in 2012, 51 in 2013 and 59 in 2014) sent by 12 partners. Around 85% of the requests received by Morocco came from France.

405. Between 2012 and 2014, the EOI requests to which Morocco responded within 90 days, within 180 days, within one year or later are expressed as percentages in the table below:

		2012		2013		2014		Total	
		Num.	%	Num.	%	Num.	%	Num.	%
Total number of requests received	(a+b+c+d+e)	72	100%	51	100%	59	100%	182	100%
Full response : ≤ 90 days		6	8%	13	26%	11	19%	30	17%
≤ 180 days (total)		10	13%	17	33%	17	29%	43	24%
≤ 1 year (total)	(a)	18	25%	25	49%	33	56%	76	42%
> 1 year	(b)	18	25%	16	31%	14	24%	48	26%
Declined for valid reasons	(c)	0	0%	0	0%	0	0%	0	0%
Failure to obtain and provide the requested information	(d)	2	3%	3	6%	2	3%	7	4%
Requests still pending at the date of review	(e)	34	47%	7	14%	10	17%	51	28%

* Morocco counts each written request from a treaty partner as a request even when the EOI request covers a number of elements of information. However, when Morocco receives a request covering more than one person, it reports it as one request per person.

** The times shown in this table are calculated from the date the request is received to the date the full and definitive response is sent.

406. Statistics provided by Morocco show that it has generally been unable to respond to EOI requests from its partners within appropriate timeframes. During the review period, Morocco provided responses to its partners within 90 days of receipt of their request in just 17% of cases. Morocco's response rate is only 42% after one year. For 26% of requests, a response was only provided after one year had elapsed. Lastly, 51 requests were still pending at the review date, which represents 28% of requests received.

407. Nevertheless, these results can partly be attributed to 2012, where Morocco was only able to process 53% of EOI requests received and where the less-than-90-day response rate was just 8%. Morocco explained these

results by the setting up of the EOI process in 2012 following its membership to the Global Forum. If the results from 2012 are not taken into consideration, Morocco's capacity to provide the required information in a timely manner improves, as shown in the table below for 2013 and 2014.

		2013		2014		Total	
		Num.	%	Num.	%	Num.	%
Total number of requests received	(a+b+c+d+e)	51	100%	59	100%	110	100%
Full response : ≤ 90 days		13	26%	11	19%	24	22%
≤ 180 days (total)		17	33%	17	29%	34	31%
≤ 1 year (total)	(a)	25	49%	33	56%	58	53%
> 1 year	(b)	16	31%	14	24%	30	27%
Declined for valid reasons	(c)	0	0%	0	0.0%	0	0%
Failure to obtain and provide the requested information	(d)	3	6%	2	3%	5	5%
Requests still pending at the date of review	(e)	7	14%	10	17%	17	15%

This trend is confirmed for 2015, which follows on from the review period and during which time Morocco was able to respond within 90 days, 180 days and less than one year to 33%, 65% and 84% of requests received, respectively.

408. The comments received from peers confirm that Morocco was generally unable to provide the required information in a timely manner during the review period. Responses to EOI requests were rarely provided within 90 days of the receipt of the request, and only sometimes within 180 days. Morocco's particularly long response times do not apply to any specific category of information. In addition, the requesting jurisdictions were not informed of the status of their request when Morocco was unable to provide a response within 90 days of receiving it, including when they reminded Morocco about it.

409. The use of information-gathering powers does not seem to be the cause of the difficulties encountered by Morocco in answering EOI requests from its partners. Indeed, the Moroccan authorities indicated that the information requested could be gathered immediately, where said information is available from the databases of the DGI, and within a timeframe of a few days or a month when the information is in a taxpayer's physical file. However, when the tax administration must use its right to information, the time allowed for the information holder to respond was, until 1 January 2016, set by the tax administration according to the degree of urgency attributed to the requested information. An explanation for Morocco's inability to provide the required information in a timely manner during the review period is therefore undoubtedly to be found in the complex EOI organisation in

Morocco, in the inadequate management of this activity, in the EOI processes put in place and in the resources allocated to it (see C.5.2 below).

410. The recent improvement in response times from Morocco, which was confirmed by the peers, is partly due to the modest improvements made in monitoring EOI requests, such as for example, the inclusion in the EOI request tracking table of a column showing when the 90-day timeframe is being exceeded. This allows a reminder to be sent to the departments in charge of gathering or sending the information to the Moroccan competent authority. However, exceeding the 90-day timeframe does not mean that a status update is sent to the requesting jurisdiction. Similarly, the implementation since 1 January 2016 of a set timeframe of 30 days for the holders of the requested information to respond to right to information notices is likely to accelerate processing of EOI requests. Nevertheless, these improvements seem inadequate for improving the time taken to respond to EOI requests.

411. In conclusion, over the review period, Morocco was only occasionally able to provide timely responses to its partners. Thus, the 90-day response rate is just 17%; only 42% of requests from Morocco's partners received a response within a year, and 28% of requests are still awaiting a response. In addition, Morocco does not inform its partners of the status of their requests when it fails to provide the information within 90 days of receipt of the request, including when a reminder has been received. Thus, over the review period, Morocco failed to obtain and provide the information requested in 7 cases and EOI requests are still pending in 51 cases. Thus, 58 EOI requests from peers received no response over this period. Peers also indicated that around 15 files were closed as a result of the information being provided too late to be of use. Morocco is therefore recommended both to ensure that it responds to all EOI requests from its partners within 90 days of receipt of them, and where this is not possible, that a status update be systematically provided.

Organisational process and resources *(ToR C.5.2)*

The Moroccan competent authority

412. The competent authority with regards to tax conventions and EOI agreements signed by Morocco is the Minister of Finances or his authorised representative. Pursuant to the decree no. 517.15 of the Minister of Finances of 12 February 2015, the Director-General of Taxes has full delegated powers with regards to receiving, processing and responding to all EOI requests for tax purposes issued by Morocco's EOI partners, as well as issuing EOI requests to Morocco's EOI partners, receiving their responses and using the content, in line with the terms of the agreements currently in force.

413. The Director-General of Taxes has delegated his authority to six managers from two different departments of the DGI, each of whom has a specific role in the EOI process. Within these two departments, officers carry out the operational functions of the competent authority within a hierarchical approach.

414. Within the Department of Legislation, Studies and International Cooperation (*Direction de la Législation, des Études et de la Coopération Internationale*, DLECI), the competent authorities are the Director, the Head of the International Cooperation Division (*Division de la Coopération Internationale*, DCI) and the Head of the International Tax Agreements Department (*Service des Conventions Fiscales Internationales,* SCFI). The four officers of the SCFI, whose duties are not entirely limited to information exchange, are qualified in international taxation and speak foreign languages, particularly English and French. Their main activity is to negotiate tax agreements and monitor their implementation. With regards to information exchange, the SCFI is in charge of:

- Ensuring the validity of incoming EOI requests and, where necessary, translating them before sending them to the SREF; and
- Examining responses to EOI requests before they are sent out via the hierarchical channels to the competent authority of the EOI partner jurisdictions.

The SCFI has the material resources needed to perform its duties (internet access, telephone, fax, and scanner) in conditions that allow it to ensure that confidential data is protected (a safe and locked filing cabinets).

415. Within the Tax Investigation Directorate (*Direction du Contrôle Fiscal,* DCF), the competent authorities are the Director, the Head of the DPRM and the Head of the SREF. In addition to its Head, the SREF also has two office managers. There are also two officers working in the BRR in Casablanca. The 5 officers of the SREF, whose duties are not entirely limited to information exchange, are qualified to gather and process information and have access to all the internal and external databases of the DGI. With regards to information exchange, the SREF is in charge of processing the EOI requests from EOI partners that have been validated by the SCFI by:

- Gathering or organising the gathering of the requested information;
- Preparing draft responses;
- Sending responses via the hierarchical channels to the competent authority in the requesting jurisdictions.

The SREF also has the material resources needed to perform its duties (internet access, telephone, fax, and scanner) in conditions that allow it to ensure that confidential data is protected (a safe and locked filing cabinets).

416. Morocco has also indicated that in recent years, the DGI systematically requires new recruits to undergo initial training which includes a module on international taxation, that includes notably tax convention and international administrative co-operation matters.

417. The Moroccan competent authorities are easily identifiable by their foreign counterparts. Their contact information is included and updated in the database of competent authorities made available to its members by the Global Forum on Transparency and Exchange of Information for Tax Purposes. In addition, Morocco has also indicated that it informs its foreign partners of any changes to the identity or contact information of the competent authorities.

418. A new organisation chart of the DGI was established by the decree no. 2.16.031 of 16 March 2016 and the decision no. 113.16 of the Minister of Finance of 17 March 2016. A unit dedicated to the exchange of information should be put in place, which will simplify the EOI organisation and circuit, notably with a significant reduction in the number of officers acting as the competent authority. Thus the operational functions of the competent authority will be centralised within the DLECI. Within this department, a new International Exchange of Information Department (*Service des Échanges de Renseignements Internationaux,* SERI), which will be located within the Taxation and International Cooperation Division (*Division de la Fiscalité et de la Coopération Internationale,* DFCI), will be the EOI unit for Morocco. As such, it will perform the functions described above, which are currently performed by the SREF and the SCFI. In addition to the department head, it will include three officers entirely dedicated to the exchange of information.

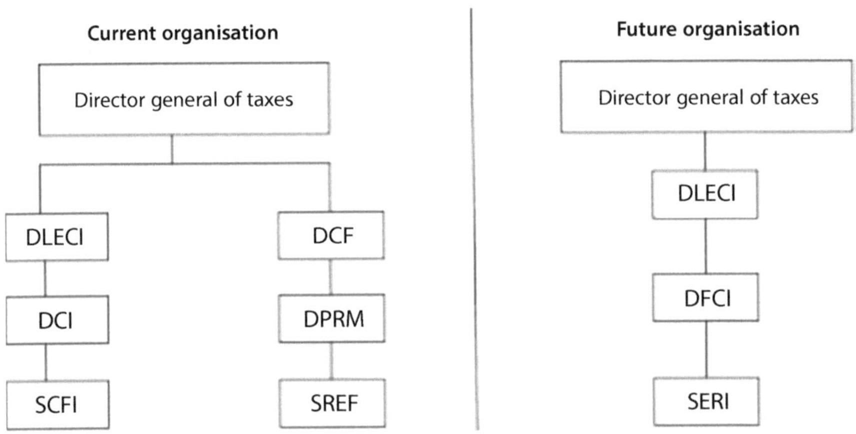

The Moroccan authorities have indicated that as soon as this structure is effectively in place, it will inform all its partners of the new identity and contact details of the Moroccan competent authority and will update the Global Forum's database of competent authorities.

The information exchange process

419. EOI requests can be sent to the competent authority of Morocco either by mail or by email. When the EOI request is sent by mail, it is received by the Central Dispatch Office (*Bureau d'Ordre Central*, BOC), where two assistants work on behalf of the Director General of Taxes. They open the mail, date it and stamp it as confidential. However, Morocco does not acknowledge receipt of EOI requests from its partners. The mail is then taken to the Director General of Taxes, whose office is adjacent to the BOC. The Director General of Taxes familiarises himself with the request and transfers it to the DLECI (copy of the EOI request) and the DCF (original EOI request) to process it at the same time. The EOI request is transferred via the internal postal system by an officer carrying a file containing the letter in an envelope, and it is handed in person to the respective directors of the DLECI and the DCF against a receipt. EOI requests are then transmitted via the same procedure to the heads of the DCI and the DRPM, then to the SCFI and the SREF. Although Morocco has not received any EOI request by email to date, the following procedure would be followed in this case: the receiving competent authority would transfer the email to the head of the SCFI and the SREF and would also print the EOI request which would follow the same circuit described for EOI requests received by mail.

420. The SCFI examines the validity of the request. In concrete terms, it ensures that the form and substance requirements of the EOI procedure have been met. In particularly, it ensures there is a legal instrument in force allowing the exchange of information with the requesting jurisdiction, and the status of competent authority of the person making the EOI request. Where necessary, the request is translated. The foreseeable relevance of the request is also verified. During the review period, Morocco did not decline any requests. The SCFI indicated that there was a broad appreciation of the foreseeable relevance of a request, and this if ever a request did not appear to be foreseeably relevant, the SCFI would immediately contact the competent authority of the requesting jurisdiction to obtain additional information, while respecting the measures of the EOI agreement. Once the demand has been validated, the SCFI informs the SREF so that they can gather the information requested.

421. The head of the SREF registers the EOI request in the Excel tracking table as soon as this has been handed to him via the internal post system. This tracking table was put in place in 2005 and a copy is archived each month in the SREF. It allows the head of the SREF to monitor requests and

response times. As mentioned earlier, at the end of 2015 the tracking table was enhanced with the addition of an indicator showing when the 90 day period had been exceeded, which allows the SREF to immediately send a reminder to the territorial departments of the DGI – the BRR or the relevant DRI department – that have failed to provide the requested information. The SREF has also access to the following indicators: the number of requests received, processed and pending and the time taken to process them.

422. After having registered the EOI request, the SREF identifies the person targeted by the EOI request, and then gathers the required information. In practice, there are three ways of gathering this information:

- When the information required is held in the databases to which the DGI has access, the SREF can gather the information directly, as it has full and complete access to all the internal databases (SIT, the national income tax files, corporation tax, etc.) and external databases of the DGI (OMPIC, ANCCF, etc.) described in section B.1 of this report. In this case, the information is immediately gathered in order to prepare the response from the Moroccan competent authority.
- When the information is available from the territorial departments of the DGI, the SREF directly contacts by email the relevant department of the DRI to obtain the information they hold, such as the taxpayer's physical file. It takes the department between a few days and a month to gather the information, depending on whether the information is in the physical file or has been archived. Once gathered, the information is provided to the SREF by email or by hand.
- When the information is not available within the DGI, the SREF uses its two officers working in the BRR in Casablanca to gather the information from the public administrations or from third parties, whether in Casablanca or elsewhere in Morocco, generally using the right to information. To this end, an email is sent to these officers containing the EOI request. The officers prepare the right to information notice(s) that they hand-deliver to the holder(s) of the information (Rabat-Casablanca area) or sent by mail (elsewhere in the Kingdom). The responses to the right to information notice are either handed to the officers of the BRR by the holder of the information on their own premises, or are sent by post to the BRR. The time needed to gather this information varies. Before 1 January 2016, the time allowed to the information holder to respond to the right to information notice from the tax authorities was set by the tax authorities according to the urgency of the request. Since 1 January 2016, the information holder must respond within 30 days of receiving the right to information notice.

423. Once the information has been collected, the SREF prepares a draft response to the EOI request. This draft response is then sent to the SCFI for approval. The SCFI ensures that the draft response is complete and that it responds to the request made by the requesting jurisdiction. If the response is approved by the SCFI, the SREF can submit the response for signature by one of the six competent authorities who will then send it to the competent authority of the partner jurisdiction.

424. The DGI does not currently have an EOI manual detailing the procedures to follow and the timeframe to respect, as well as the diligences and the precautions that must be taken when processing EOI requests. The operations described above do not have predefined timeframes, and they are not documented. The Moroccan authorities have indicated that a general DGI procedures manual is in the process of being written. This manual will contain a section on the procedures to follow when dealing with EOI requests and will be updated to illustrate the organisation changes relating to exchange of information.

425. Over the review period, Morocco received 182 EOI requests but was unable to provide the information requested in a timely manner, as explained above. Despite the high number of EOI requests, the EOI process was dealt with in an ad hoc manner, involving a number of departments that were not dedicated specifically to this task. Thus, as a result of the complex organisation, inadequate steering, non-documented processes, and particularly the lack of a EOI manual and a timeframe for each stage of the EOI process, as well as the non-dedicated resources, Morocco was unable to process EOI requests from its partners efficiently and a timely manner. The procedure for processing EOI requests involves too many people, who are not entirely allocated to this task and who report to different hierarchical chains of command. The imminent implementation of a dedicated structure and the distribution of a DGI general procedural manual including a section on exchange of information, which is currently being written, will no doubt lead to an improvement in the processing of EOI requests. Morocco is recommended to put in place a suitable organisation and monitoring system for the processing of EOI requests from its partners, in particularly by adopting internal deadlines for processing requests and a documented process, in order to ensure that in all cases, partners receive timely responses to their requests.

Lack of restrictive conditions on exchange of information (ToR C.5.3)

426. There is no provision in Moroccan legislation or in its EOI agreements which contains specific conditions governing the exchange of information, other than those included in Article 26 of the OECD Model Convention or the OECD Model TIEA. In practice, no condition likely to limit the exchange of information was noted.

Conclusion and factors underlying the recommendations

Phase 1 determination
This element involves issues of practice that are assessed in the Phase 2 review. Accordingly no Phase 1 determination has been made.

Phase 2 rating	
Partially compliant.	
Factors underlying the recommendation	**Recommendation**
Over the review period, Morocco was only occasionally able to provide timely responses to its partners. Thus, the 90-day response rate is just 17%; only 42% of requests from Morocco's partners received a response within a year, and 28% of requests are still awaiting a response. However, Morocco improved its response times immediately after the review period and this progress should improve further with the implementation of an EOI unit and the publication of an EOI manual.	Morocco should ensure that it responds in a timely manner to all EOI requests from its EOI partners.
Over the review period, Morocco did not inform its EOI partners of the status of their requests when it failed to provide the information within 90 days of receipt of the request, sometimes including when a reminder has been received.	Morocco should systematically provide a status update to its EOI partners in situations when the competent authority is unable to provide a response within 90 days of receipt of the request.
Over the review period, despite the high number of EOI requests, the EOI process was dealt with in an ad hoc manner, involving a number of departments that were not dedicated specifically to this task. Thus, as a result of the complex organisation, inadequate steering, non-documented processes and non-dedicated resources, Morocco was unable to process the EOI requests from its partners efficiently and in a timely manner. However, Morocco has recently approved the creation of a dedicated EOI unit and an EOI manual is in the process of being written, which should improve the way EOI requests are processed.	Morocco should accelerate the implementation of a suitable organisation and monitoring system for the processing of EOI requests from its partners, in particularly by adopting internal deadlines for processing requests and a documented process, in order to ensure that in all cases, EOI partners receive timely responses to their requests.

Summary of conclusions and factors underlying recommendations

Overall Rating
LARGELY COMPLIANT

Conclusion	Factors underlying the recommendations	Recommendations
Jurisdictions should ensure that ownership and identity information for all relevant entities and arrangements is available to their competent authorities. *(ToR A.1.)*		
Phase 1 conclusion: The element is in place but certain aspects of the legal implementation of the element need improvement.	Only limited companies and partnerships limited by shares can legally issue bearer shares in Morocco, which represents less than 9% of companies with share capital. Of these, only those that expressly included this possibility in their articles of association can issue such shares. The examination by the Moroccan authorities of the articles of association of all limited companies and partnerships limited by shares did not identify any companies that had included this option in their articles of association. Although a review of corporate records did not reveal that any bearer shares had been issued or were in circulation in Morocco, Morocco still allows limited companies and limited partners of partnerships limited by shares to issue them without having introduced arrangements whereby their holders can be identified under all circumstances.	Morocco should take the necessary measures to ensure that appropriate arrangements are in place such that the holders of bearer shares can be identified under all circumstances.

Conclusion	Factors underlying the recommendations	Recommendations
Phase 1 conclusion: The element is in place but certain aspects of the legal implementation of the element need improvement. *(continued)*	There are no penalties to enforce the obligation for limited companies, which represent less than 9% of companies with share capital in Morocco, to maintain a share register and the obligation, for companies, to file and keep the originals of correspondence received and copies of correspondence sent.	Morocco should ensure that penalties exist in all cases for non-compliance with legal provisions relating to the identification of the owners of relevant entities.
Phase 2 rating: Partially compliant.		
Jurisdictions should ensure that reliable accounting records are kept for all relevant entities and arrangements. *(ToR A.2.)*		
Phase 1 conclusion: The element is in place but certain aspects of the legal implementation of the element should be improved.	According to Moroccan laws, accounting records and supporting documentation must be kept for 10 years. However, there is no direct sanction for failure to respect this obligation, although dissuasive tax sanctions can be applied in this case. However, given the time-bar rules, the sanction for failure to keep accounting records or supporting documents beyond the four years of the time-bar is not guaranteed in certain situations.	Morocco must ensure that appropriate sanctions are applicable in all cases for non-compliance with the requirement to keep accounting records including supporting documentation for at least five years.
Phase 2 rating: Largely compliant.		
Banking information should be available for all account-holders. *(ToR A.3.)*		
Phase 1 conclusion: The element is in place.		
Phase 2 rating: Compliant.		

Conclusion	Factors underlying the recommendations	Recommendations
Competent authorities should have the power to obtain and provide information that is the subject of a request under an exchange of information arrangement from any person within their territorial jurisdiction who is in possession or control of such information (irrespective of any legal obligation on such person to maintain the secrecy of the information). *(ToR B.1.)*		
Phase 1 conclusion: The element is in place.		
Phase 2 rating: Largely Compliant.	During the review period, the right to information of the tax administration, which is its main power to obtain information from third parties, did not include a compulsory time limit to reply. Moreover, the sanctions applicable for failure to respond to the right to information were not dissuasive. However, the provision relating to the right to information has been modified recently. Since 1 January 2016, the right to information includes a compulsory 30-day time limit to reply and dissuasive sanctions.	Morocco should monitor the effective application of the new provisions regarding the right to information in practice.
The rights and safeguards (e.g. notification, appeal rights) that apply to persons in the requested jurisdiction should be compatible with effective exchange of information. *(ToR B.2.)*		
Phase 1 conclusion: The element is in place.		
Phase 2 rating: Compliant.		
Exchange of information mechanisms should provide for effective exchange of information. *(ToR C.1.)*		
Phase 1 conclusion: The element is in place, but certain aspects of the legal implementation of the element should be improved.	8 of the tax agreements signed by Morocco before 2014 as well as the Multilateral Convention signed on 21 May 2013, which offers Morocco 54 potential new EOI partners, are still not in force in Morocco.	Morocco must ensure that the EOI agreements it signs enter into force rapidly.

Conclusion	Factors underlying the recommendations	Recommendations
Phase 2 rating: Largely compliant.		
The jurisdictions' network of information exchange mechanisms should cover all relevant partners. *(ToR C.2.)*		
Phase 1 conclusion: The element is in place.		Morocco should continue to extend its EOI network in compliance with the standard.
Phase 2 rating: Compliant.		
The jurisdictions' mechanisms for exchange of information should have adequate provisions to ensure the confidentiality of information received. *(ToR C.3.)*		
Phase 1 conclusion: The element is in place.		
Phase 2 rating: Compliant.		
The exchange of information mechanisms should respect the rights and safeguards of taxpayers and third parties. *(ToR C.4.)*		
Phase 1 conclusion: The element is in place.		
Phase 2 rating: Compliant.		
The jurisdiction should provide information under its network of agreements in a timely manner. *(ToR C.5.)*		
This element involves issues of practice that are assessed in the Phase 2 review. Accordingly no Phase 1 determination has been made.		

Conclusion	Factors underlying the recommendations	Recommendations
Phase 2 rating: Partially compliant.	Over the review period, Morocco was only occasionally able to provide timely responses to its partners. Thus, the 90-day response rate is just 17%; only 42% of requests from Morocco's partners received a response within a year, and 28% of requests are still awaiting a response. However, Morocco improved its response times immediately after the review period and this progress should improve further with the implementation of an EOI unit and the publication of an EOI manual.	Morocco should ensure that it responds in a timely manner to all EOI requests from its EOI partners.
	Over the review period, Morocco did not inform its EOI partners of the status of their requests when it failed to provide the information within 90 days of receipt of the request, sometimes including when a reminder has been received.	Morocco should systematically provide a status update to its EOI partners in situations when the competent authority is unable to provide a response within 90 days of receipt of the request.
	Over the review period, despite the high number of EOI requests, the EOI process was dealt with in an ad hoc manner, involving a number of departments that were not dedicated specifically to this task. Thus, as a result of the complex organisation, inadequate steering, non-documented processes and non-dedicated resources, Morocco was unable to process the EOI requests from its partners efficiently and in a timely manner. However, Morocco has recently approved the creation of a dedicated EOI unit and an EOI manual is in the process of being written, which should improve the way EOI requests are processed.	Morocco should accelerate the implementation of a suitable organisation and monitoring system for the processing of EOI requests from its partners, in particularly by adopting internal deadlines for processing requests and a documented process, in order to ensure that in all cases, EOI partners receive timely responses to their requests.

Annex 1: Jurisdiction's response to the review report[16]

Le Maroc présente ses remerciements au secrétariat du Forum mondial et au Forum mondial dans son ensemble pour leur assistance et leur accompagnement dans la conduite de son évaluation par les pairs.

Le Maroc souhaite également exprimer sa gratitude à l'équipe d'évaluation pour le travail considérable qu'elle a effectué et pour avoir guidé le Maroc de façon constructive durant la phase 2 de son évaluation par les pairs.

Le Maroc remercie pareillement les membres du Peer Review Group ainsi que ses autres partenaires en matière d'échange de renseignements pour leurs contributions et commentaires pertinents durant son évaluation.

Enfin, le Maroc qui prend très au sérieux les recommandations énoncées dans le rapport, souhaite réitérer son engagement dans la mise en place du standard de l'échange de renseignement sur demande et assure ainsi les membres du Forum mondial que les efforts seront doublés afin de satisfaire au plus vite lesdites recommandations.

16. This Annex presents the jurisdiction's response to the review report and shall not be deemed to represent the Global Forum's views.

Annex 2 : List of all exchange of information mechanisms in force

Exchange of information agreements signed by Morocco as at 1 July 2016, in alphabetical order.

Morocco signed the Multilateral Convention, as amended, on 21 May 2013 but not yet ratified it.

	Jurisdiction	Type of agreement	Signature [a]/ Territorial scope	Date of entry into force/Status
1	Albania	Double taxation treaty	5 October 2015	Not in force
		Multilateral Convention	Signed	In force in Albania
2	Algeria	Arab Maghreb Union tax convention	23 July 1990	14 July 1993
3	Andorra	Multilateral Convention	Signed	Not in force
4	Anguilla [b]	Multilateral Convention	Extended	In force in Anguilla
5	Argentina	Multilateral Convention	Signed	In force in Argentina
6	Aruba [c]	Multilateral Convention	Extended	In force in Aruba
7	Australia	Multilateral Convention	Signed	In force in Australia
8	Austria	Double taxation treaty	27 February 2002	12 November 2006
		Multilateral Convention	Signed	In force in Austria
9	Azerbaijan	Multilateral Convention	Signed	In force in Azerbaijan
10	Bahrain	Double taxation treaty	7 April 2000	10 February 2001
11	Barbados	Multilateral Convention	Signed	Not in force
12	Belgium	Double taxation treaty (revised)	31 May 2006	30 April 2009
		Multilateral Convention	Signed	Convention in force in Belgium
13	Belize	Multilateral Convention	Signed	In force in Belize

	Jurisdiction	Type of agreement	Signature[a]/ Territorial scope	Date of entry into force/Status
14	Bermuda[b]	Multilateral Convention	Extended	In force in Bermuda
15	Brazil	Multilateral Convention	Signed	Not in force
16	British Virgin Islands[b]	Multilateral Convention	Extended	In force in the British Virgin Islands
17	Bulgaria	Double taxation treaty	22 May 1996	6 December 1999
		Multilateral Convention	Signed	In force in Bulgaria
18	Burkina Faso	Double taxation treaty	18 May 2012	Not in force
19	Cameroon	Double taxation treaty	7 September 2012	Not in force
		Multilateral Convention	Signed	In force in Cameroon
20	Canada	Double taxation treaty	22 December 1975	9 November 1978
		Multilateral Convention	Signed	In force in Canada
21	Cayman Islands[b]	Multilateral Convention	Extended	In force in the Cayman Islands
22	Chile	Multilateral Convention	Signed	Not in force
23	China (People's Republic of)	Double taxation treaty	27 August 2002	16 August 2006
		Multilateral Convention	Signed	In force in China (People's Republic of)
24	Colombia	Multilateral Convention	Signed	In force in Colombia
25	Costa Rica	Multilateral Convention	Signed	In force in Costa Rica
26	Côte d'Ivoire	Double taxation treaty	20 July 2006	7 March 2016
27	Croatia	Double taxation treaty	26 June 2008	25 October 2012
		Multilateral Convention	Signed	1 June 2014
28	Curaçao[c]	Multilateral Convention	Extended	In force in Curaçao
29	Cyprus[e]	Multilateral Convention	Signed	In force in Cyprus
30	Czech Republic	Double taxation treaty	11 June 2001	18 July 2006
		Multilateral Convention	Signed	In force in Czech Republic
31	Denmark	Double taxation treaty	8 May 1984	25 December 1992
		Multilateral Convention	Signed	In force in Denmark

	Jurisdiction	Type of agreement	Signature [a]/ Territorial scope	Date of entry into force/Status
32	Dominican Republic	Multilateral Convention	Signed	Not in force
33	Egypt	Double taxation treaty	22 March 1989	28 May 1993
34	El Salvador	Multilateral Convention	Signed	Not in force
35	Estonia	Double taxation treaty	25 September 2013	Not in force
		Multilateral Convention	Signed	In force in Estonia
36	Faroe Islands [d]	Multilateral Convention	Extended	In force in the Faroe Islands
37	Finland	Double taxation treaty (revised)	7 April 2006	20 October 2012
		Multilateral Convention	Signed	In force in Finland
38	Former Yugoslav Republic of Macedonia (FYROM)	Double taxation treaty	11 May 2010	14 September 2012
39	France	Double taxation treaty	29 May 1970	1 December 1971
		Amendment	18 August 1989	1 December 1992
		Multilateral Convention	Signed	In force in France
40	Gabon	Double taxation treaty	3 June 1999	16 May 2008
		Multilateral Convention	Signed	Not in force
41	Georgia	Multilateral Convention	Signed	In force in Georgia
42	Germany	Double taxation treaty	7 June 1972	8 October 1974
		Multilateral Convention	Signed	In force in Germany
43	Ghana	Multilateral Convention	Signed	In force in Ghana
44	Gibraltar [b]	Multilateral Convention	Extended	In force in Gibraltar
45	Greece	Double taxation treaty	20 March 2007	17 November 2010
		Multilateral Convention	Signed	In force in Greece
46	Greenland [d]	Multilateral Convention	Extended	In force in Greenland
47	Guatemala	Multilateral Convention	Signed	Not in force
48	Guernsey [b]	Multilateral Convention	Extended	In force in Guernsey
49	Guinea	Double taxation treaty	3 March 2014	15 January 2016
50	Guinea-Bissau	Double taxation treaty	28 May 2015	Not in force
51	Hungary	Double taxation treaty	12 December 1991	20 August 2000
		Multilateral Convention	Signed	In force in Hungary
52	Iceland	Multilateral Convention	Signed	In force in Iceland

	Jurisdiction	Type of agreement	Signature[a]/ Territorial scope	Date of entry into force/Status
53	India	Double taxation treaty	30 October 1998	20 February 2000
		Amendment	8 August 2013	Not in force
		Multilateral Convention	Signed	In force in India
54	Indonesia	Double taxation treaty	8 June 2008	10 April 2012
		Multilateral Convention	Signed	In force in Indonesia
55	Iran	Double taxation treaty	25 February 2008	Not in force
56	Ireland	Double taxation treaty	22 June 2010	31 August 2012
		Multilateral Convention	Signed	In force in Ireland
57	Isle of Man[b]	Multilateral Convention	Extended	In force on the Isle of Man
58	Israel	Multilateral Convention	Signed	Not in force
59	Italy	Double taxation treaty	7 June 1972	10 March 1983
		Protocol	28 May 1979	10 March 1983
		Multilateral Convention	Signed	In force in Italy
60	Jamaica	Multilateral Convention	Signed	Not in force
61	Japan	Multilateral Convention	Signed	In force in Japan
62	Jersey[b]	Multilateral Convention	Extended	In force in Jersey
63	Jordan	Double taxation treaty	16 May 2005	26 March 2009
64	Kazakhstan	Multilateral Convention	Signed	In force in Kazakhstan
65	Kenya	Multilateral Convention	Signed	Not in force
66	Kuwait	Double taxation treaty	16 May 2002	15 July 2006
67	Latvia	Double taxation treaty	24 July 2008	25 September 2012
		Multilateral Convention	Signed	In force in Latvia
68	Lebanon	Double taxation treaty	20 October 2001	7 August 2003
69	Libya	Arab Maghreb Union tax convention	23 July 1990	14 July 1993
70	Liechtenstein	Multilateral Convention	Signed	Not in force
71	Lithuania	Double taxation treaty	19 April 2013	Not in force
		Multilateral Convention	Signed	In force in Lithuania
72	Luxembourg	Double taxation treaty	19 December 1980	16 February 1984
		Multilateral Convention	Signed	In force in Luxembourg

	Jurisdiction	Type of agreement	Signature [a]/ Territorial scope	Date of entry into force/Status
73	Malaysia	Double taxation treaty	2 July 2001	31 December 2006
74	Mali	Double taxation treaty	20 February 2014	3 June 2016
75	Malta	Double taxation treaty	26 October 2001	15 June 2007
		Multilateral Convention	Signed	In force in Malta
76	Mauritania	Arab Maghreb Union tax convention	23 July 1990	14 July 1993
77	Mauritius	Double taxation treaty	25 November 2015	Not in force
		Multilateral Convention	Signed	In force in Mauritius
78	Mexico	Multilateral Convention	Signed	In force in Mexico
79	Moldova	Multilateral Convention	Signed	In force in Moldova
80	Monaco	Multilateral Convention	Signed	Not in force
81	Montserrat[b]	Multilateral Convention	Extended	In force in Montserrat
82	Nauru	Multilateral Convention	Signed	Not in force
83	Netherlands	Double taxation treaty	12 August 1977	10 June 1987
		Multilateral Convention	Signed	In force in Netherlands
84	New Zealand	Multilateral Convention	Signed	In force in New Zealand
85	Nigeria	Multilateral Convention	Signed	In force in Nigeria
86	Niue	Multilateral Convention	Signed	Not in force
87	Norway	Double taxation treaty	5 May 1972	18 December 1975
		Multilateral Convention	Signed	In force in Norway
88	Oman	Double taxation treaty	15 December 2006	22 April 2009
89	Pakistan	Double taxation treaty	18 May 2006	8 October 2009
90	Philippines	Multilateral Convention	Signed	
91	Poland	Double taxation treaty	24 October 1994	22 August 1996
		Multilateral Convention	Signed	In force in Poland
92	Portugal	Double taxation treaty	29 September 1997	27 June 2000
		Multilateral Convention	Signed	In force in Portugal
93	Qatar	Double taxation treaty	17 March 2006	8 May 2009
		Double taxation treaty (revised)	27 December 2013	
94	Romania	Double taxation treaty	2 July 2003	16 August 2006
		Multilateral Convention	Signed	In force in Romania

	Jurisdiction	Type of agreement	Signature[a]/ Territorial scope	Date of entry into force/Status
95	Russia	Double taxation treaty	4 September 1997	20 September 1999
		Multilateral Convention	Signed	In force in Russia
96	Saint-Maarten[c]	Multilateral Convention	Extended	In force in Saint-Maarten
97	San Marino	Multilateral Convention	Signed	In force in San Marino
98	Sao Tome and-Principe	Double taxation treaty	25 January 2016	
99	Saudi Arabia	Double taxation treaty	14 April 2015	Not in force
		Multilateral Convention	Signed	In force in Saudi Arabia
100	Senegal	Double taxation treaty	1 March 2002	19 May 2006
		Multilateral Convention	Signed	Not in force
101	Serbia	Double taxation treaty	6 June 2013	Not in force
102	Seychelles	Multilateral Convention	Signed	In force in the Seychelles
103	Singapore	Double taxation treaty	9 January 2007	15 January 2014
		Multilateral Convention	Signed	In force in Singapore
104	Slovak Republic	Multilateral Convention	Signed	In force in Slovak Republic
105	Slovenia	Double taxation treaty	5 April 2016	Not in force
		Multilateral Convention	Signed	In force in Slovenia
106	South Africa	Multilateral Convention	Signed	In force in South Africa
107	South Korea	Double taxation treaty	27 January 1999	16 June 2000
108	Spain	Double taxation treaty	10 July 1978	16 May 1985
		Multilateral Convention	Signed	In force in Spain
109	Sweden	Multilateral Convention	Signed	In force in Sweden
110	Switzerland	Multilateral Convention	Signed	Not in force
		Double taxation treaty	31 March 1993	27 July 1995
111	Syria	Double taxation treaty	19 June 2005	25 March 2009
112	Tunisia	Arab Maghreb Union tax convention	23 July 1990	14 July 1993
		Multilateral Convention	Signed	In force in Tunisia

	Jurisdiction	Type of agreement	Signature[a]/ Territorial scope	Date of entry into force/Status
113	Turkey	Double taxation treaty	7 April 2004	18 July 2006
		Multilateral Convention	Signed	Not in force
114	Turks and Caicos Islands[b]	Multilateral Convention	Extended	In force in the Turks and Caicos Islands
115	Uganda	Multilateral Convention	Signed	Not in force
116	Ukraine	Double taxation treaty	13 July 2007	3 March 2009
		Multilateral Convention	Signed	In force in Ukraine
117	United Arab Emirates	Double taxation treaty	9 February 1999	2 July 2000
118	United Kingdom	Double taxation treaty	8 September 1981	28 November 1991
		Multilateral Convention	Signed	In force in United Kingdom
119	United States	Double taxation treaty	1 August 1977	1 January 1981
120	Uruguay	Multilateral Convention	Signed	Not in force
121	Viet Nam	Double taxation treaty	24 November 2008	12 September 2012
122	Yemen	Double taxation treaty	8 February 2006	Not in force

Notes: a. For signature dates of the Multilateral Convention, see: www.oecd.org/ctp/exchange-of-tax-information/Status_of_convention.pdf.

b. Territorial extension by the United Kingdom.

c. Territorial extension by the Kingdom of the Netherlands.

d. Territorial extension by the Kingdom of Denmark.

e. Footnote by Turkey: The information in this document with reference to "Cyprus" relates to the southern part of the Island. There is no single authority representing both Turkish and Greek Cypriot people on the Island. Turkey recognises the Turkish Republic of Northern Cyprus (TRNC). Until a lasting and equitable solution is found within the context of United Nations, Turkey shall preserve its position concerning the "Cyprus issue".

Footnote by all the European Union Member States of the OECD and the European Union: The Republic of Cyprus is recognised by all members of the United Nations with the exception of Turkey. The information in this document relates to the area under the effective control of the Government of the Republic of Cyprus.

Annex 3: List of all laws, regulations and other material received

Commercial legislation

Commercial Code

Dahir on obligations and contracts

Dahir 1-58-376 of 15 November 1958 regulating the right of association as amended and supplemented

Act 17-95 on limited companies as amended by Acts 81-99 and 20-05

Act 5-96 on partnerships, limited liability companies and joint ventures as amended by Acts 82-99, 21-05 and 24-10

Act 9-88 on accounting requirements for traders

Tax legislation

Tax Code

Anti-money laundering legislation

Act 43-05 on money-laundering

Financial legislation

Act 34-03 on credit institutions and similar organisations

Act 58-90 on offshore financial centres

Other

Finance Ministry order, OJ no. 3949 of 6 July 1988

Penal Code

Dahir 1-58-008 of 24 February 1958 on the civil service regulations

Dahir enacting Act 1-93-62 of 10 September 1993 organising exercise of the legal profession

Decree no. 2-89-591 of 4 December 1989, OJ no. 4024 of 20 December 1989Act 35-96 on the creation of a central depositary and the institution of a general rule for the registration in accounts of certain securities

Act 32-09 organising the notarial profession

ORGANISATION FOR ECONOMIC CO-OPERATION AND DEVELOPMENT

The OECD is a unique forum where governments work together to address the economic, social and environmental challenges of globalisation. The OECD is also at the forefront of efforts to understand and to help governments respond to new developments and concerns, such as corporate governance, the information economy and the challenges of an ageing population. The Organisation provides a setting where governments can compare policy experiences, seek answers to common problems, identify good practice and work to co-ordinate domestic and international policies.

The OECD member countries are: Australia, Austria, Belgium, Canada, Chile, the Czech Republic, Denmark, Estonia, Finland, France, Germany, Greece, Hungary, Iceland, Ireland, Israel, Italy, Japan, Korea, Latvia, Luxembourg, Mexico, the Netherlands, New Zealand, Norway, Poland, Portugal, the Slovak Republic, Slovenia, Spain, Sweden, Switzerland, Turkey, the United Kingdom and the United States. The European Union takes part in the work of the OECD.

OECD Publishing disseminates widely the results of the Organisation's statistics gathering and research on economic, social and environmental issues, as well as the conventions, guidelines and standards agreed by its members.

OECD PUBLISHING, 2, rue André-Pascal, 75775 PARIS CEDEX 16
(23 2016 45 1 P) ISBN 978-92-64-26105-1– 2016

www.ingramcontent.com/pod-product-compliance
Ingram Content Group UK Ltd.
Pitfield, Milton Keynes, MK11 3LW, UK
UKHW060018051026
15591UKWH00003B/254
* 9 7 8 9 2 6 4 2 6 1 0 5 1 *